The Peaceful Cook

more than a cookbook

by
Harriet Kofalk

The Book Publishing Company
Summertown, Tennessee

Cover design and illustration by Byron Allen,
inspired by Melissa Verbena

We gratefully acknowledge the use of following previously copywritten material:
pg. 145, **We're All Doing Time,** by Bo Lozoff, Human Kindness Foundation, Durham,
NC, 1985, pg. 146, Excerpted from **Staying Healthy with The Seasons,** copyright ©1981
by Elson Hass, M.D. reprinted by permisssion of Celestial Arts, Berkeley, CA, pg. 146,
Truth or Dare , by Starhawk, Harper & Row, 1987, pg. 147, **Bread in Time— Breadbaking Without Angst,** by Stuart Silverstein, Robin Hood Books, Knox via Brooks, ME,
1990, pg. 147, **The Sexual Politics of Meat: A Feminist—Vegetarian Critical Theory,**
by Carol J. Adams. Reprinted by permission of The Continuum Publishing Company,
pg. 147, **Food Is Your Best Medicine,** by Dr. Henry G. Bieler, Random House, New
York, NY, 1965, pg. 148, **Your Health Your Choice,** by Dr. M. Ted Morter, Jr., Fell
Publishers, Hollywood, FL, 1990, pg. 149, **The Runoff,** by Patricia Robinett, Many
Rivers Group division of the Oregon Chapter of the Sierra Club, Eugene OR, 1990, pg.
150, **The Art of Good Living-Sinple Steps to Regaining Health and the Joy of Life,** by
Svevo Brooks, Houghton Mifflin, Boston, MA, 1990, pg. 157, **What Is A Vegetarian?** by
the Braham Kumaris World Spiritual Organization, Los Angeles CA, (reprinted from
the Raja Yoga Center in London, England), pg. 151, **Cooking with Spirit—North
American Food and Fact,** by Darcy Williamson and Lisa Railsback, Maverick Publica-
tions, Bend, OR, 1988

Library of Congress Cataloging-in-Publication Data
Kofalk, Harriet, 1937-
The peaceful cook : more than a cookbook / by Harriet Kofalk.—
1st ed.
    p. cm.
    Includes index.
    ISBN 0-913990-46-9
    1. Vegetarian cookery. 2. Vegetarianism. I. Title.
TX837.K64 1991
641.5'636—dc20   92-41331
                                                                    CIP

ISBN 0-913990-46-1

A portion of the proceeds
from this book supports
the activities of
Peace Place

Printed on recycled paper
so the forests and wildlife may share
more peaceful homes with us.

Dedication

Dedicated to Ellen, the original "Peaceful Cook," a dear soul sister. The principles she taught me have helped to create this book. Not only the physical body, but also the mind, emotions, and subtle body are greatly affected by the consciousness in which food has been prepared. When this intangible influence is taken into consideration, food preparation becomes more than the process of merely creating tasty, nourishing meals; it becomes an act of spiritual responsibility to those who will eat that food, including oneself.

In addition, I'd like to acknowledge all the books and all the cooks who have led this cook to become more peaceful by creating that consciousness. A special thanks goes to those who have enjoyed experimenting by eating these creations, including those who attend our weekly vegetarian cooking class, "The Peaceful Cook." And the ultimate thanks goes to our mother/father spiritual guide in whose universe we live and move and have our being—in peace.

Corn Mother

As I plant the seeds
in the warm earth
the scent of spring
still hangs in the air

they sprout
into the miracle of life
in the summer sun
and grow
into tall stalks
with flowers
nurtured
by the melody of bees

soon small ears appear
to grow within
the tight cocoons
lined with silk
and the long leaves rustle
in the first autumn breeze
to signal
the beginning
of their harvest time
when they emerge
into the fullness
of their nature
before they rest
in the silence
of waiting
to give birth

—h.k.

Table of Contents

Introduction

Peace is a power within, and we who spend time in the kitchen can reconnect with peace there. The power we use to feed ourselves provides a very simple beginning to creating more peace in our lives. Paying attention—being mindful—is a key that can unlock that power of peace. In the kitchen we can choose to be in touch with that place within ourselves where we feel peace.

Food is to our bodies what thoughts are to our minds—the fuel that feeds our souls. By paying attention to our food we create power-full fuel for our bodies; we become reconnected with food as the source of our physical well-being. We can then reconnect with its source—and ultimately our own—in the universe. We begin to understand our own place in the continuum of life, as well as to experience the interconnectedness of all creation. We can then digest our food more deeply and use it more effectively, just as we use our thoughts more deeply, more effectively, when we are aware of their focus and aim and interconnections.

Consider a dish of applesauce. When we pick apples from a tree that we have watched grow and ripen through the seasons and then cook that fruit, it tastes different from fruit that we buy in a can. Apples that we buy from the farmer who grew them taste different from those in a supermarket that have been trucked or flown hundreds or thousands of miles to the store (not to mention the amount of non-renewable energy it takes to transport them!). And picking an apple from your own tree that has not been poisoned with pecticides and gassed to give it longer shelf life increases your connection with the Earth.

This is not to suggest that we all go "back to the land" but simply become more conscious of the food we eat and its source. One time to do this is as we pick or buy it. Another is as we prepare it to eat.

The simple act of cutting an apple can become a meditation—a process of using our thoughts in a more focused way. As I wash the apple, I marvel at its color and texture, the sunshine that ripened it, the many leaves on the tree that helped it grow, the nutrients from the soil that are its essence as well. As I cut the apple, I see its whole life story: the skin that encases it, the flesh that surrounds and feeds the seeds that create the next generation, the blossom end that was its flower, the stem that held it firm to its parent tree. And I haven't even tasted the apple yet.

To "cook" in the sense of the "peaceful cook" means to create an awareness of the power of peace within. Heat has long been known as a purifier, and the most powerful moment in the preparation of food is when it is put to the fire—be it the stove, the oven, the toaster, or whatever. As we pay attention at this time and are mindful of the flame purifying the food, changing it, we bring more awareness during the rest of the process, especially if that is given the priority it deserves in our lives.

The atmosphere in the kitchen during food preparation is an important aspect of peaceful cooking. We can begin by focusing on one meal a day to honor the preparation. First, we can check within, and if necessary, refocus our mind so that the cooking is envisioned as an enjoyable, creative activity. We can check the environment to be sure the kitchen is clean and in order, so the process of cooking is smoother. We can avoid being distracted by other work or by the telephone. (Let it ring and see how empowering that feels.) By giving attention to the task at hand we can create an entirely new atmosphere in which to work *simply by paying attention*. Then the kitchen can become peaceful from our own inner power of peace. This will actually save time, and the food will definitely turn out better. This is one way peace can emerge in the world, and it begins in our own kitchen.

Once the food is prepared, another aspect of peaceful cooking is to honor that food. Some do this by saying grace, or by holding hands around the table, or by having those present each say thanks in their own way. My personal practice is to put a small amount of the freshly cooked food in a small container, place it on a small trivet and cover it with a clean cloth. Then I sit in silent meditation with it for several minutes, honoring its source and mine, and the use to which this food will go. If I am sharing the meal, as is often the case, all present join me in this celebration. This ceremonial food is then returned to the pot from which it came, so all who share the food share the energy that has been given to it. In this way, the dining area too can become peace-full from our own power of peace.

A wonderful word I discovered while researching this book is "commensality." It means "eating together." German sociologist Max Weber emphasized that commensality "effectively cements social relationships." Increasingly I value our *sense of community—* whoever we are who gather together. When we celebrate life by commensality, especially a meal that we create ourselves, we strengthen our sense of community.

Simply sharing food together is a way of being good to ourselves as well as to our friends and family. On a more practical level, by eating at home we can avoid the 80% of food-borne illness that can be traced to restaurant eating (reported in *Modern Maturity* magazine, June 1991). *The Peaceful Cook* provides many opportunities to create celebrations with food at home. In fact, it exists because that has happened. For more than two years I've taught a class called "The Peaceful Cook." The class is designed to empower people to cook and eat more creatively, more consciously, more healthfully. And we share who we are in the process.

New Orleans chef Leah Chase said once, "You have to be in love with that pot. You have to put all your love in that pot. If you're in a hurry, just eat your sandwich and go. Don't even start cooking, because you can't do anything well in a hurry." That does not mean we have to spend a lot of time cooking. In fact, we can create more voluntary simplicity in our lives by spending overall no more time preparing food than eating it. *The Peaceful Cook* is dedicated to this principle. Time and energy to enjoy our food thus becomes an added benefit.

These steps don't happen overnight—although they can. Each is a purposeful beginning. We can each take one small step that feels right for our own circumstances. If the goal is to become a more peaceful cook, the next step will always be waiting in the wings for our readiness to take it. For the moment, my friend, sit quietly and visualize your kitchen, your dining area, your food, with the power of peace described above. Does it feel good? What step can you take *now* to create that scene in your own life?

Do it, now.

Perhaps, just perhaps, that powerful place of peace within is the seed from which the world tree of peace can grow.

Credo

Cooking peacefully is more a state of mind than it is the ingredients used, although part of the process of creating that state of mind includes paying attention to the ingredients. *The Peaceful Cook* is based on a lacto-vegetarian diet because that is my personal practice as a peaceful cook, and I can only write about what I know. I use dairy products (less and less as time goes on), but no other animal products (meat, poultry, fish or eggs). I use rennetless cheese because the coagulant rennet is made from the lining of calf stomachs. I also use agar, a product derived from seaweed, instead of gelatin, which is made from animal hooves.

The Peaceful Cook is more than a cookbook. Each page contains two elements besides a recipe:

View of the Whole—something to think about while preparing that dish. This can help to instill the habit of focusing on the food and its preparation rather than on other things while in the kitchen.

Embracing Mother Earth—an Earth-related comment about an ingredient, such as a gardening tip or other ways to use the ingredient.

This provides both an Earthly and a spiritual connection for every dish. They can help you to develop your own peaceful process, whatever food you prepare. When we give our Earth a mental hug each time we prepare a meal, and remember that she too is a symbol for the larger universe we share, we reconnect with the basic values of a peace-full life. This creates more peace that we then infuse in the foods we prepare.

Let's review some basic principles before we get into the recipes.

Much literature is available on various forms of vegetarianism these days, so I leave that discussion to others. My own vegetarian diet has stood me well for several years, and I write from that experience. A section at the back of the book, "As Others Say It," contains comments by other authors to encourage you further.

The more I learn about people who are survivors of major diseases like cancer, the more I see the connections between disease and eating processed foods and the more I become interested in eating raw fruits and vegetables. Dr. Ted Morter (in "As Others Say It" at the back of the book) recommends that 75% of our diet be fruits and vegetables, half of them eaten raw and half eaten cooked. Our body can then handle anything we eat for the other 25%. He particularly recommends starting each meal with something raw. This starts enzyme action which promotes better digestion.

Here is a list of choices, in descending order of preference, that I use to obtain fruits and vegetables.

1. Grow it yourself, organically. Then you know how and where it grows.

2. Buy organic produce from a local farmer. If organic produce is not available, select IPM (integrated pest management) foods from a local grower whose farming principles you know and agree with. This supports growers working in harmony with the Earth and you could make a new friend. It also gets the message out that we want to buy from local people, especially from those who are healing the Earth.

3. Buy organic foods from a reputable natural foods store whose food buyers know the growers they buy from.

4. Buy locally grown produce from other sources.

5. Shop at a large commercial supermarket only if there is no other option.

Once this choice is made, wherever I obtain produce I "listen" to the food. As I attune myself more to fresh foods, they "speak" to me and I can more effectively select those who are ready to come home with me.

Some of the principles followed in *The Peaceful Cook*:

1. Eat locally produced foods in season. This is an important key to good health, and buying food grown locally—what we do not grow ourselves—also helps our neighbors. The recipes in this book are arranged seasonally to encourage this choice and to

suggest a time of year to serve each dish. This principle also serves as a reminder of the cyclical nature of time and the overlapping seasons of life.

2. Spend no more time overall in preparing food than in eating it. The few recipes in this book that take more energy are balanced with those that take less.

3. Think simplicity. We can be nourished more by simplicity than by complexity, in foods as well as in other aspects of our lives. Each set of facing pages is a main course and a dessert that balance each other. Simple one-dish meals are appropriate for our busy times and the demands on our energy.

4. In place of water in a recipe (from another source), use vegetable stock; in desserts use fruit juice and reduce the amount of sweetener. Vegetable stock can be made from the stems, skins and other less edible portions of organic vegetables and some fruit, which can be saved in a container in the refrigerator. Every few days put these in a pot, along with any leftover cooking water from steaming vegetables, and cover with water. Bring to a boil and simmer for about 20 minutes. Strain the resulting liquid and refrigerate until needed. Only make stock in this way with organic produce to avoid consuming the essence of pesticides. As a side benefit, the cooked-down ends then compost more quickly when put in the garden.

5. Use lots of apples in cooking. The preponderance of apple recipes in this cookbook speaks not only of the magnificent grandfather Gravenstein apple tree outside my window, but of the benefits of apples to our health. The apple tree is known in many cultures as the "tree of life." Apple pectin is a digestive aid, and a fresh-picked organic apple eaten before a meal is hard to beat as an enzyme stimulator.

6. Limit the use of processed food. I use butter instead of margarine because I believe the benefits outweigh the disadvantages, especially if we are careful about other fat in our diet. Butter works well for greasing baking pans. It blends with the food rather than forming a sticky film that is difficult to remove. If you are concerned about cholesterol, many dishes can be made with half (or all) unrefined vegetable oil in place of butter, but the result will be different. When butter is replaced

by oil in a dessert recipe, a small amout of sea salt will liven the flavor. Oil should always be used instead of butter when sautéing over high heat.

7. Instead of salt (except as mentioned above), I use Bragg's Liquid Aminos. This 75-year-old natural unfermented soy product offers a balanced blend of amino acids, and it also replaces soy sauce or tamari (which is aged soy). A squirt of Bragg's in a cup of hot vegetable stock or water also makes a good soup.

8. Use strong spices in moderation. I use nothing in the onion/garlic family. These are stimulants, much like caffeine, and can negatively affect the subtlety of our internal processes. Many other items can take the place of these popular ingredients, and my digestion and health have never been better.

There are no rules in this game of food preperation. In the final analysis, listen to your own body. As you become more sensitive to your food, your body will talk to you more directly and you will learn to listen to it more directly—and become more peace-full in the process. You will know this through your sense of inner joy, for joy is the result of peace. EnJOY!

Summer

Mustard
grows tall in the garden
flowers
support the bees
and tell me
it's summer
time to grow
tall in the garden
flowering
supporting
telling my story
spiced
with the blossoms
of the mustard
seeds
of faith

-h.k.

Blender Gazpacho

View of the Whole

Cold soup is an appealing part of summer dinners. The name gazpacho and this particular blend of ingredients are common to our neighbors to the south. Honor their presence on the planet as a part of honoring this meal, and thank them too for sharing these ideas with us.

½ green pepper
3 tomatoes
1½ cucumbers or medium zucchini
½ cup cold vegetable stock or water
3 Tbsp. rice vinegar
½ tsp. chili pepper
2 Tbsp. vegetable oil
1 tsp. Bragg's Liquid Aminos

Slice or quarter vegetables, setting aside half a cucumber or zucchini for a garnish. Put into blender and blend 3 seconds or until cucumber is shredded. Mix all ingredients in a bowl and refrigerate until serving time. Finely chop ½ cucumber or zucchini for garnish.
Serves 6 as side dish, 4 as main dish.

Options:
Fresh corn tortillas go well with this soup. Heat a dry heavy skillet until hot. Put in one tortilla at a time, turning after 30 seconds (or as soon as it is soft and warm). Warm the same amount of time on the other side. Stack in a covered bowl or in a towel to keep warm until served. Caution: Tortillas will get tough if heated too long; keep warming time to a minimum.

Embracing Mother Earth

This soup gathers all of summer's favorite colors and textures in one bowl and blends them into an appetizing whole. Other available fresh vegetables may also be added. Blending them allows you almost an infinite choice of ingredients. Enjoy!

Fresh Grape Pie

View of the Whole

*By being aware of the workers who grow and pick our fruits
we can connect our energy with them as we prepare foods like this,
and thus cooperate subtly in the healing of our Earth.*

3 Tbsp. cornstarch	1 quart seedless grapes,
¾ cup fruit juice	or other fresh fruit in
¼ cup honey	bite-size pieces
1 Tbsp. fresh lemon juice	1 tsp. vanilla
grated peel of one lemon	1 cup yogurt or sour cream

Mix cornstarch, fruit juice, and honey in a pan. Boil until thick and clear, approximately 5 minutes. Add lemon juice and peel, and pour mixture over grapes in pie crust. Chill. Before serving, mix vanilla (and a little honey, if desired) into yogurt and spread on pie.

Walnut Crust

1 cup whole wheat pastry flour
¼ cup walnuts, chopped
¼ tsp. baking powder
¼ tsp. sea salt
2 tsp. cinnamon
2 Tbsp. honey
3 Tbsp. unrefined vegetable oil

Combine the dry ingredients. Gradually add honey and oil, and mix well. Press mixture into a buttered 9" deep dish pie plate. Bake 12-14 minutes at 350° or until golden brown. Cool until ready to use.
Serve 6-8.

Embracing Mother Earth

*In summer, remember to bake when the house can cool off,
such as late evening. Conversely, in cold weather bake when you want the house
warmer, such as early morning, and get double use from the oven's heat.
Enjoy it all!*

Joyce's Friday Night Couscous

View of the Whole

Cooking couscous is deceptively simple, another advantage during busy days. Cooking is like other parts of life: we forget how simple it can be when we take time to notice and appreciate it. The kitchen is a good place to remember the basic simplicity of life's ingredients.

For couscous:
1¼ cups vegetable stock or
  water
2 Tbsp. unrefined vegetable oil
1 cup whole wheat couscous

For sauce:
1 Tbsp. unrefined vegetable oil
¼ large yellow or red sweet
  pepper, chopped
6-8 tomatillos*, chopped
1 tsp. ground cumin

For couscous: Bring stock and oil to a boil. Add couscous, lower heat and simmer five minutes. Cover and let sit for five additional minutes. Fluff with fork and serve.

For sauce: Heat oil in skillet. Sauté vegetables until soft; add cumin. Cover and let steam for 2-3 minutes. Add cooked couscous and mix. Or serve vegetables over the couscous.
Serves 3-4.

Options:
Chopped fresh tomato and jicama* are also good additions.

> *Tomatillos are a South-of-the-border variety of tomatoes that are easy to grow and produce an abundant crop of small, crisp-flavored, green fruits. They are good raw in salads, simmered in sauce like this one or in a salsa for Mexican dishes.*
> *Jicama are beet-shaped root vegetables with crisp white flesh. They can be eaten raw or cooked.*

Embracing Mother Earth

*As we experiment and enjoy various ingredients like the unfamiliar tomatillos, we begin to remember and honor the biodiversity of the planet we share.
We are then less likely to take unconscious actions that go counter to that respect.
Left over couscous can be served as a breakfast cereal, heated with raisins and nuts, or sautéed and used as a side dish for another dinner. Mix it cold with chopped salad vegetables and dress with unrefined vegetable oil and rice vinegar for lunch.
You spend no more time preparing Friday Night Couscous than eating it, so enjoy it even more!*

Lemon Cookies

View of the Whole

Sweets have traditionally been a "reward" for eating one's dinner. When we eat them consciously, with the thought that they are reminders to keep our words sweet, they take on a new significance. Effective reminders are not heavy and not excessive; a small one serves well. These cookies make excellent reminders. Enjoy them in this understanding.

⅓ cup raisins
3 Tbsp. apple or other
   fruit juice
1 Tbsp. honey
½ cup butter
grated rind of one lemon
2 tsp. fresh lemon juice
1 cup whole wheat pastry
   flour
½ cup nuts, chopped
¼ cup sunflowers seeds

Purée raisins with apple juice in blender. Combine raisin purée, honey, butter, lemon juice and rind. Add flour, nuts and seeds, and mix gently. Form into walnut-sized balls and place on buttered cookie sheet. Press with thumb to flatten slightly. Bake at 350° for 10-12 minutes or until lightly browned. Remove from oven and cool on cookie rack.
Makes 2 dozen.

Embracing Mother Earth

*Nutrition is not just a matter of biochemistry; it also involves our connections with food. We can become more conscious of those connections with food and the Earth by using fresh local ingredients. The original recipe called for frozen apple-juice concentrate and no honey. In season, fresh apple juice is best; even freshly frozen is better than commercially produced frozen. You can experiment with varying the sweetener to taste, keeping the amount of liquid the same.
Enjoy!*

Tofu Curry Dip, Etc.

View of the Whole

Just as the best recipes are the simplest, the best combinations of our creative thoughts are also the simplest and easiest to understand. We can ponder similarities like this productively, while blending the spices of our own creative juices--be it in cooking or in other endeavors.

1 cup tofu, cut in small pieces
1 tsp. lemon juice
2 Tbsp. rice vinegar
1 tsp. Bragg's Liquid Aminos
1 Tbsp. unrefined vegetable oil
1½ tsp. curry powder
1 tsp. Dijon mustard

Put all ingredients in a blender and mix until smooth.
Serves 4

Options:

This can be used as a salad dressing on fresh greens, as a dip for fresh vegetables, or as a sandwich spread.

Embracing Mother Earth

Plan to keep a fresh lemon on hand, especially an organically grown one. The scent of lemon on your fingers after grating the peel or squeezing the juice adds a nutritive value to your psyche that no yellow plastic container can match. One trade-off is that lemons are not locally grown in many places, so are trans- ported great distances. But the advantage is that fresh lemons bring you closer to the Earth.
Enjoy!

Scrumptious Biscuits

View of the Whole

Cooking biscuits is a time-honored tradition. They are so easy to make and so tasty it's hard to imagine why canned ones are so popular. Whatever kind of biscuits you choose to make, be conscious of the energy involved. It takes little of your energy, but requires a hot oven. When possible, combine oven tasks. Bake cookies or something else while you have that heat generating. Also be conscious of the heat as a way to burn off questions inside you. They will be answered by the self-respect gained from participating actively in preparing your own food.

2½ cups whole wheat pastry flour
1 Tbsp. baking powder
¾ cup milk
1 Tbsp. honey
½ cup melted butter
fresh fruit, if used as shortcake

In a large mixing bowl, combine flour and baking powder. Gently mix in other ingredients, using a wooden spoon. Pat dough out on a floured surface until about 1" thick. Cut out biscuits with a small juice glass or jelly jar (makes about 20), or with a biscuit cutter (makes about 12). Bake at 400° for 25-30 minutes, or until golden brown.

For Shortcake: Break biscuits in half crosswise. Top with fresh fruit and plain yogurt, adding a few carob chips to celebrate.

Embracing Mother Earth

Picking your own strawberries is a great way to connect this recipe with our Mother Earth—and gain more appreciation for those who labor in the fields for a living. Welcome that opportunity, or select them at the store with the same connection. Both you and the berries will benefit from the respect gained.
Enjoy!

Soba with Nut Sauce

View of the Whole

*How fortunate we are to live in this day and age!
We can sample noodles from Japan, nuts from across the country,
and the simple pleasures of eating together in peace. While it's important to focus
more attention on local ingredients and supporting local growers, it's also
important to appreciate the whole planet we share. A balance of the two brings a
glow to our lives that embraces who we really are.*

**8 oz. soba or somen noodles (buckwheat noodles)
1 cup walnuts (or pecans if you crave richness)
1 cup vegetable stock or water
3 Tbsp. sweet white miso paste,
    or ¼ cup grated parmesan cheese
and ½ tsp. Bragg's Liquid Aminos**

Heat a large pot of water to boiling and cook noodles only until they become limp (3-5 minutes). Drain and set aside.

Roast nuts in a dry skillet over medium heat, stirring constantly until they are crisp and fragrant. Blend them with miso and stock in a blender until smooth, adding more liquid if needed. Toss noodles with sauce and top with a fresh mushroom slice, if desired.
Serves 4, with a green salad.

Embracing Mother Earth

*We tend to think of pasta as spaghetti, but many forms of pasta abound worldwide.
It's fun to experiment with different ones and learn to taste their differences,
enjoying the whole.*

Raita (Fruit with Sauce)

View of the Whole

Fresh fruit in any form "freshens" a meal.
As we pay attention to the fresh thoughts that occur to us
and act on them, we move more into our own inner peaceful place.
A good time to think about this is while cutting fruit.
It creates fresh ideas, and imparts love in the food we are preparing.

3-4 whole, fresh seasonal fruits
¼ cup sour cream
¼ cup yogurt
1 Tbsp. honey
1 tsp. ground cardamom

Select a mixture of 3-4 whole, fresh seasonal fruits (approximately 1 cup per person). Cut into bite-size pieces. If fruits that darken quickly are used (apples, some pears, bananas), sprinkle with fresh lemon juice. Set aside.

Combine sour cream and yogurt (or all yogurt) with honey and ground cardamom. Mix sauce gently with fruit, and refrigerate until serving time. *Serves 4.*

Embracing Mother Earth

Minerals are concentrated near the skins of fruit.
Another advantage of organically grown fruit is you can eat the skins
without concern for what's been sprayed on them. When they haven't been gassed
or treated chemically, they taste much better.
Enjoy!

Sesame Vegetable Rice

View of the Whole

*Whether it's the summer weather that encourages easy cooking
or simply your schedule, brown rice and vegetables make a comfortable, quick
main meal. Preparation takes little energy, leaving you better able to focus on
participating in the process. Everyone gains—you as cook, your family
(or your own stomach) as consumers, and the planet.*

1 cup brown rice, cooked (see below)
unrefined vegetable oil, as needed
2-3 cups thinly sliced mixed vegetables (whatever is in season or
  available: carrots, celery, broccoli, squash, cabbage, beans,
  mushrooms)
¼ cup sesame seeds
1 Tbsp. Bragg's Liquid Aminos

To cook rice: Bring rice to a boil in 2 cups of vegetable stock or
water. Lower heat to simmer, cover and cook 45 minutes. Let it stand 10
minutes before serving. When the rice is almost ready, toast sesame seeds
in a dry, heavy skillet over medium heat until they brown and smell fragrant.
Set them aside in a small bowl.

In the same skillet sauté vegetables in 1 Tbsp. oil, beginning with those that
take longest to cook (carrots, broccoli, cabbage). You can also stir-fry them
with a small amount of liquid, covered. Do not overcook; vegetables are
ready when crisp and heated through.

Serve vegetables on rice, sprinkled with sesame seeds and topped with liquid
aminos to taste.
Serves 4.

Embracing Mother Earth

*One of the joys of cooking is to use what's available.
Feel a sense of well-being by not putting energy into finding what to fix,
but by fixing what you find. This recipe allows you complete latitude to do
just that and to celebrate the rainbow of vegetables that can be combined.
Enjoy!*

Halva–Indian Style

View of the Whole

It's satisfying to envision a complete meal with balanced ingredients. When the main course is rice and vegetables, you can top it off with a richer, dairy-based dessert like this. Satisfying our inner needs by envisioning our wholeness adds richness to our inner life as well.

½ cup butter
1½ cups farina (cream of wheat or cream of rice)
4 cups milk
3-6 cardamom pods, ground,
 or grated peel of one orange
½ cup raisins
a few drops of vanilla or almond extract
¼ cup slivered almonds
2 Tbsp. honey

Melt butter over low heat in skillet. Add farina and heat for several minutes, stirring and taking care not to burn it. Add milk and stir well. Add other ingredients except honey. Stir until the mixture comes away from the sides of the pan, approximately 5-10 minutes. Add honey and stir.
Serves 6.

Options:

You can serve this warm in individual dishes. You can also put it in the oven at a low temperature, with a lid, to hold until time to serve. Or you can spread it in a greased baking tray, flatten it like candy and refrigerate, cutting it into squares or diamonds to serve cold—makes 3 dozen.

Embracing Mother Earth

When baking something to be refrigerated, let it cool to room temperature first. Then the refrigerator doesn't have to work so hard to cool it, saving energy. Sharing and talking about recipes from other countries is one way to increase cultural awareness and enjoy the fruits of all our timeless labors. This simple recipe has many variations from many cultures. And it takes little energy to create. Enjoy!

Summer White Bean Soup

View of the Whole

A complete meal in itself, this dish reminds us of how we too combine various ingredients to become whole.

1 cup dried white beans
8 cups vegetable stock or water
1 bay leaf
½ cup chopped celery or Swiss chard stems
1 Tbsp. unrefined vegetable oil
1 quart washed and chopped Swiss chard leaves
1 Tbsp. Bragg's Liquid Aminos
3 Tbsp. rice vinegar

Cover the beans with water and soak for 6-8 hours, or overnight. (In hot weather, put the soaking beans in the refrigerator to keep them from fermenting.) Before cooking, drain and combine beans with vegetable stock, or fresh water, and bay leaf. Bring to a boil and simmer for 1½ hours, or until
tender.

In a skillet, sauté celery in oil and add to beans with other ingredients. Cook until chard is tender but still bright green, about 5-10 minutes. Remove bay leaf.
Serves 4.

Embracing Mother Earth

Cook this in the evening, so the house can cool overnight.
Flavors blend better with time and you can quickly reheat it for dinner the next night. If you grow Swiss chard, the stems easily replace celery and make full use of the garden produce.
Enjoy!

Almond Fool

View of the Whole

Food balance includes the whole meal, not just the main course.
When serving a light meal, a stronger dessert may be in order.
(This one is a "fooler," for it contains no saturated fat and lots of nutrition,
blending well-soaked almonds instead of whipped cream.)
Because it's easy to make and requires no heat, it's especially good
for hot summer nights. And it provides contentment for the cook,
who labors with love, as well as for the eaters,
who are well nurtured by the process as well as by the ingredients.

⅓ cup raw almonds
1 cup water
1 Tbsp. honey
½ tsp. vanilla
½ tsp. cinnamon
chilled, puréed fruit in season

Soak almonds in water for 24 hours, or at least overnight. Put the soaked almonds and ⅔ cup soaking water in a blender with honey, vanilla and whatever spice is compatible with fruit to be used. Blend until smooth and fluffy. Pour into bowl and chill in refrigerator.

In a blender purée enough fruit to equal half the almond mixture. Chill fruit in a separate bowl. To serve, spoon almond mixture into serving dishes and top with fruit purée.
Serves 4.

Options:
Experiment with various combinations of spices and fruits. Cinnamon with peaches is good, and topping with a few fresh blueberries for decoration is even better. You can also use the almond mixture without the fruit as a topping for fruit pies and puddings.

Embracing Mother Earth

Air steals vitamins, so purée the fruit as near to serving time as
possible while giving it time to cool. Nuts other than almonds
may be used but none is as high in nutrition. Another way to save
energy is to use the same blender container for the fruit as you did
for the almonds. No need to wash it in between; the flavors blend well.
Enjoy!

Mary's Salad

View of the Whole

*This salad is like eating rainbows. Broccoli is one of the
most nutritious vegetables. Combining its deep green with bright peppers and a
root vegetable like carrots provides a balanced set of salad ingredients.
Garbanzo beans add protein, making the salad a full meal. As one physician
advised, "If your plate is colorful, you're getting a well balanced diet."*

**3 cups total (in a proportion to suit your taste)
  carrots, broccoli, red and green peppers
1 cup sprouted garbanzo beans
2 Tbsp. unrefined vegetable oil
1 Tbsp. rice vinegar
1 tsp. basil
½ cup grated cheese (optional)**

Cut vegetables in bite-size pieces. Add sprouted garbanzo beans, and toss
with oil, vinegar and basil. Sprinkle with grated cheese just before serving,
if you choose.
Serves 3.

Options:
The sprouted beans can also be ground in a blender with oil, vinegar, herbs, and
other ingredients such as green chilis, ripe olives and Dijon mustard. Use as a
sandwich spread.

Embracing Mother Earth

*Instead of canned beans, try making your own sprouted beans.
Nothing could be simpler. They taste better, are more nutritious,
and are much cheaper. The beans expand 3-4 times, so plan accordingly.
Put dry beans in a container several times larger than they are and add warm water
a couple inches over their tops. Cover the container loosely. Let stand overnight;
then drain off water. (Use it to water plants—it's very nutritious.)
Remove cover to rinse beans with warm water 2-3 times a day for several days,
until sprouts are an inch long and start to show green as leaves form.
Refrigerate. They can be eaten as is. If you prefer, you can then steam
them 20-30 minutes, until tender. Drain and add the dressing described above.
Marinate until ready to make the salad.
Enjoy!*

Ceremonial Cornbread

View of the Whole

*Some Native Americans consider corn the symbol
of humanity—each kernel a person, the ear joining together all.
In the Southwest, Native Americans honor the Corn Mother.
Blue corn is used for ceremonial purposes,
sprinkled on passing dancers at the start of a ritual
and left at shrines as ritual food when prayer feathers are planted.*

**1¾ cups unprocessed cornmeal
1 tsp. baking soda
¾ cup whole wheat pastry flour
1 tsp. baking powder
½ cup unrefined vegetable oil
1 cup buttermilk or sour milk
1-2 Tbsp. honey
1 cup yogurt
1 Tbsp. Bragg's Liquid Aminos**

Preheat oven to 350°. In a large bowl stir together dry ingredients, then add liquids. Mix lightly and pour into a buttered 9" x 9" baking pan. Place pan in the oven slowly, honoring the process and the energy being used to prepare the food. Bake 30-45 minutes, until cornbread is light brown on top and doesn't "talk back" when you listen to it. (You can hear it cooking if it's not yet done.)

Options:
Depending on what you're serving it with, add ½ cup raisins (reduce honey to 1 Tbsp.), or replace 2 Tbsp. of the cornmeal with blue cornmeal to add a ceremonial touch. Try adding 1 cup shredded cheddar cheese (reduce milk by ½ cup), perhaps with ¼ cup chopped green chili or ½ tsp. chili powder.

Embracing Mother Earth

*Be conscious of the value of the liquids you add to a
recipe as well as the other ingredients. Instead of using plain water, save
the broth left when cooking vegetables and use that. In the cornbread you can
also use the water left from steaming the garbanzo beans for Mary's Salad (pg. 30).
Enjoy!*

Stir-fry Delight

View of the Whole

*Simplicity is the key to it all. We've simply forgotten that. As we prepare
a meal like this and focus on its simplicity, it serves as a reminder
to us of how simple other parts of our life can be as well.*

**2 Tbsp. unrefined vegetable oil
2 fresh tomatoes, chopped
6 sliced tomatillos (small green Mexican tomatoes)
1 cup sprouted (or cooked) black beans
1 cup cooked brown rice
12 mushrooms, sliced
2 cups fresh greens or sliced zucchini
½ cup raisins
½ cup vegetable stock or water
½ cup yogurt**

Put oil in a hot skillet and stir-fry tomatoes, tomatillos, beans, rice,
mushrooms, greens and raisins. Add stock, cover and steam over high heat
for 5 minutes. When done, top with yogurt.
Serves 4.

Options:
A mixture of chopped avocado and grated cheese is a good topping alternative to
yogurt and raisins.

Embracing Mother Earth

*Tomatillos are a South-of-the-border variety of tomatoes
that are easy to grow and produce an abundant crop of crisp-flavored
green fruits. They are good raw in salads, simmered in sauce like this one or
in a salsa for Mexican dishes. Experiment—it's the spice of cooking
as well as the spice of life.
Enjoy!*

Honey Fondue

View of the Whole

*The richness of this dessert is a special treat
that goes well with a lighter meal.
It's also especially good when the meal is a relaxed one
with time to enjoy one another in quiet conversation.
The medley of fruits reminds us of the medley of good thoughts
that go into creating for ourselves a life that is a special treat.*

**1 cup butter
1 cup whipping cream
½ cup honey
½ cup thick fruit jam
1½ Tbsp. cornstarch
¼ cup fresh orange or apple juice
4 cups assorted fresh fruits, sliced or cut
into bite-size pieces to use as dippers**

Heat butter, cream, honey and jam at medium temperature until butter is melted. Reduce heat and blend in a mixture of the cornstarch and juice. Continue cooking, stirring constantly, until thickened. Sauce may be prepared ahead of time; reheat to serve.
Serve with fruit dippers to 6-8 delighted people.

Embracing Mother Earth

*What better way to honor the season, any time of year,
than to select the best seasonal fruits and prepare them as a special treat.
When organically grown fruits are used, the peels taste especially delicious
and add trace minerals to our diet. Those peels that aren't eaten add rich
compost to our garden for the next crop.
Enjoy!*

Teriyaki Tofu

View of the Whole

*How often we overlook the simple things of life,
like the ease with which this tofu main dish goes together.
Put on some brown rice to steam while fixing the teriyaki, add a fresh vegetable,
and dinner is ready—while you're still smiling and ready to serve and eat it.*

**1 lb. tofu, cut into ½ slices
2 Tbsp. fresh ginger, minced
½ cup Bragg's Liquid Aminos
2 Tbsp. lemon juice
2 tsp. honey
fresh lemon peel**

Spread tofu slices in a single layer (if possible, or turn often) in a glass or stainless steel container. Combine the remaining ingredients for a marinade; pour over tofu slices and let stand for at least 2 hours. Drain and reserve marinade.

Dip tofu slices in a mixture of ½ cup whole wheat pastry flour and ¼ tsp. black pepper. Brown slices in oil, adding more oil as needed. When all the slices are browned, reduce heat, add reserved marinade and simmer 10 minutes.
Serves 4 with rice and vegetables.

Embracing Mother Earth

*The natural beauty and flavor of these simple ingredients mingle into
a taste-tempting dinner. Using fresh ingredients such as ginger helps a lot.
No need to peel it first. Before squeezing the lemon for its juice, grate
off the outer peel and add that too. Do this whenever you use lemon juice to
increase the lemony flavor of recipes.
Enjoy!*

Fruit Pizza

View of the Whole

*When you don't find what you want, invent it! This recipe
allows the cook's individual creativity to shine. If you like mandalas or focused
designs, you can create a whole meditation around the process of pizza design.*

For dough:

**1½ tsp. dry active yeast
½ cup warm water
1½ cups unbleached white flour
½ tsp. sea salt
1 Tbsp. unrefined vegetable oil**

Dissolve yeast in warm water (test it for warmth on the inside of your wrist
as you would milk from a baby bottle). Stir in flour, salt and oil. Knead the
dough on an oiled board (not floured; oil makes the pizza dough easier to
handle) until smooth and satiny, about 3 minutes. Place dough in an oiled
bowl, cover with a damp towel and set to rise in the oven set at its lowest
temperature (no higher than 150°) until doubled in bulk, about 45 minutes.
Roll out dough until thin; spread it evenly on an oiled pan (rectangular will
work as well as round). Bake at 400° for 10 minutes or until lightly browned.

For topping: Spread dough with ¼ cup almond (or other nut) butter. Cut
2-3 kinds of fresh firm fruit into interesting bite-size pieces. Apples and pears
work well; so do bananas. Avoid too many soft fruits. Arrange fruit in an
attractive design on the almond butter. Return pizza to the oven for 5 minutes
to meld the ingredients.

*Serves 8 (less if you're still hungry from dinner, or can't resist the yeasty
scent of pizza baking).*

Embracing Mother Earth

*Creating new recipes is a wonderful way to feel good
about your food and your own abilities in the kitchen.
Enjoy!*

Pasta Salad Supreme

View of the Whole

This salad is an experiment from start to finish. You can mix any fresh vegetables you have available; just stay aware of their blend of flavors. Mild-flavored ones work best. If you like the results, write them down quickly, for they have a way of disappearing. In fact, they might not be duplicatable, given what's in most gardens and refrigerators to draw from. That's part of the fun; and cooking, like life, can always include more fun if we choose. Enjoy the whole process!

1 cup vegetable pasta per person
3-4 tomatoes (depending on size)
2 medium zucchini
4 Tbsp. unrefined vegetable oil
2 Tbsp. rice vinegar
1 tsp. basil

Experiment with shells, trumpets, spirals, and other fun shapes pasta comes in. Cook pasta 8-10 minutes in boiling water. Drain and rinse with cold water. Meanwhile, in blender, purée fresh tomatoes and zucchini. You can choose to serve this hot or cold. For cold, simply combine raw vegetables. For hot, heat purée and other chopped vegetables for a minimum time, no more than 5 minutes.

For dressing: Blend vegetable oil and rice vinegar with any herbs you like. Basil is particularly nice in this salad. Fresh herbs are better than dried. Mix dressing with other ingredients. Toss with pasta and top with grated cheese if that suits you.
Serves 4.

Options:
Examples of vegetables you might include: chopped tomatoes, zucchini, carrots, green or red peppers, mushrooms, and parsley.

Embracing Mother Earth

This salad uses the fullness of Earth's bounty in a mouth-watering array. To use the leftovers, you can add other things as you go, like fresh cherry tomatoes, chopped cucumber or part of another salad like marinated green beans or eggplant. Anything goes. And it goes fast! Enjoy!

Carob Fudge Balls

View of the Whole

*We are culturally programmed for dessert to follow meals,
or at least I was. So the trick today is to discover ways to satisfy that
inner feeling with wholesome foods. Carob is a good alternative to chocolate.
It may not satisfy the chocoholic, but we can feel better about avoiding the
stimulation of the caffeine. The other ingredients in these delicacies
certainly go a long way to satisfy most sweet-teeth. And feeling better about
ourselves is part of the fun of creating in the kitchen.*

1¼ cups toasted carob powder
⅓ cup hot water
¼ cup nut butter
2 Tbsp. honey
1 tsp. vanilla
1 cup walnuts, chopped
grated coconut (optional)

Mix the carob powder and hot water together well. Mix in other ingredients
and blend thoroughly. Form mixture into small balls; dampen your hands if
necessary to keep mix from sticking to them. Roll balls in grated coconut if
desired. Refrigerate until firm.
Makes 2-3 dozen balls.

Options:
A good Earthy addition is ¼ tsp. of mint oil.

Embracing Mother Earth

*These nut balls are quick and easy, allowing you more time to enjoy
other experiences of food preparation. The fun increases when
you involve others in the ball-rolling.
Enjoy!*

Cucumber Soup with Yogurt

View of the Whole

*This recipe arrived in my hands via Bulgaria. Often we don't know
the origin of recipes, much less the origin of our thoughts. Occasionally
it's fun to consciously trace them back as far as we can and to discover
how many connections we make along the way.*

1 quart plain yogurt
4 tsp. vegetable oil
1 lb. cucumbers, diced
½ cup walnuts, chopped
1 Tbsp. Bragg's Liquid Aminos
freshly ground pepper
chopped fresh dill

Whisk yogurt in a large bowl until smooth. Add oil and whisk to blend. Mix
in cucumbers, walnuts, liquid aminos and pepper. Top with fresh dill.
Refrigerate until serving time. May be prepared a day ahead of time so
flavors blend.
Serves 6.

Embracing Mother Earth

*Organic cucumbers do not need peeling, for their peels
are neither bitter nor waxed for shelf life. Lemon cucumbers
are especially mild and their skins are very thin.
Enjoy!*

Brian's Cookies

View of the Whole

Cooking is a time of sharing. It's also a time to ponder those who have shared recipes with us and thus become a part of our own life. Bless you, Brian, whoever and wherever you are!

1 cup soft butter
¼ cup honey
4 tsp. molasses
2 Tbsp. yogurt
2 tsp. vanilla
1 cup whole wheat pastry flour
1 cup unbleached white flour
1 tsp. baking soda
½ chopped walnuts
½ cup carob chips
¾ cup raisins
3 Tbsp. sunflower seeds
1 tsp. instant decaffeinated coffee (optional)

Cream the butter and honey until smooth. Add liquid ingredients and beat well. Mix dry ingredients together and mix them in. Fold in walnuts, carob chips, raisins, and "sunny" seeds. Drop by small spoonfuls on a buttered cookie sheet. Bake at 350° for 10-12 minutes or until lightly browned underneath.
Makes 4 dozen.

Embracing Mother Earth

Brian's original recipe included 6 oz. semi-sweet chocolate. Life is stimulating enough these days, so we are better off avoiding the caffeine that chocolate has in overabundance. Either way, enjoy!

Zucchini Sauce for Pasta

View of the Whole

*Here's a delightfully simple and delicious sauce
that gives you much freedom to enjoy a summer evening.*

**2 lbs. pasta
6 cups zucchini
3 carrots
6 Tbsp. butter
juice of ½ lemon**

Cook pasta. Slice zucchini and steam until soft, about 6 minutes. In a blender, combine with butter and lemon juice. Return to pan and heat over low heat until ready to serve. Thin-slice carrots and steam 5-10 minutes until firmly tender. Serve sauce over pasta; sprinkle with carrots. No need to serve with cheese; it contains flavor enough as it is.
Serves 6.

Embracing Mother Earth

*Zucchini growers and lovers, take note! Here's a simple way to use both
young squash and "the one that didn't get away" but just kept growing.
Enjoy!*

Sunflower Specials

View of the Whole

It would be hard to beat this cookie for simplicity. The simplest ideas can be the most profound, whether in food or in any other aspect of life. We can then take time to enjoy the blending of the simple flavors, rather than trying to guess all the complexities that are involved.

1 cup butter
1 cup honey
2½ cups whole wheat pastry flour
1 tsp. vanilla
2 cups sunflower seeds, ground in blender

Melt butter and honey in the oven while it heats to 350°. Mix in other ingredients. Drop by small spoonfuls on a buttered cookie sheet. Bake for 15 minutes.
Makes 4-5 dozen treats.

Embracing Mother Earth

Growing your own sunflowers is a wonderful way to brighten any garden space. Grown in a square, their nodding heads roof a playhouse—for the child in each of us. The birds and squirrels may find the seeds before you do, but a few remain to start the next year's crop.
Enjoy!

Elegant Spinach Casserole

View of the Whole

*Elegance and simplicity join hands in this delightfully simple recipe.
We embrace the fullness of the results even as we prepare the meal.*

2 lbs. fresh spinach or Swiss chard
1½ cups cottage cheese
3 cups grated cheddar cheese
2 cups whole wheat bread crumbs
¼ tsp. nutmeg
1 Tbsp. Bragg's Liquid Aminos
¼ tsp. black pepper

Wash the spinach well and let it drain; then chop into bite-sized pieces. (At this point you may steam it for 2 minutes to make handling it easier if you prefer.) In a 9" x 13" baking pan, layer spinach, cottage cheese, grated cheese and crumbs. Sprinkle with spices. Cover pan and bake 30-40 minutes at 350°.
Serves 6.

Embracing Mother Earth

*Freezing the ends of loaves of bread,
instead of throwing them away, saves them to use in recipes like this.
Enjoy!*

Lemon Drop Cookies

View of the Whole

Lemons leave a fresh taste in your mouth and make a great complement to any dinner. These cookies are one good way to take advantage of this feeling. Freshness in any form is valuable and a complement to the routine—a good thought to remember in communicating with words as well as food.

½ cup butter
grated peel from one lemon
½ cup honey
2¼ cups whole wheat pastry flour
1 cup yogurt
1 tsp. baking soda
⅓ cup lemon juice
½ cup chopped walnuts, or poppy seeds (optional)

While heating the oven to 350°, use it to melt together butter and honey. Blend in yogurt, lemon juice and peel. Mix the flour and soda in well. Stir in nuts or seeds. Drop by small spoonfuls on a buttered cookie sheet. Bake 15 minutes or until lightly browned.
Makes 4 dozen cookies.

Embracing Mother Earth

This recipe takes advantage of the whole lemon. Pulp is a strong flavoring agent all too often left out of recipes. It feels good to include the whole lemon and to see the smiles of those who sniff the freshly baked cookies with anticipation. Enjoy!

Squash Delight

View of the Whole

The best recipes, like the best thoughts, turn up in the moment and are not necessarily planned or anticipated. The discovery becomes part of the process and the joy, be it of cooking or of contemplating.

4 yellow crookneck squash or medium zucchini
2 stalks celery, chopped
1 green or yellow pepper, chopped
½ cup milk
6 slices jack or cheddar cheese
1 tsp. chili pepper

Slice squash thinly and place in casserole dish. Add celery and pepper; pour in milk. Top with cheese and sprinkle with chili pepper. Cover and bake at 375° for 30-45 minutes.
Serves 3-4 as side dish, or 2 as main dish on top of baked potatoes.

Embracing Mother Earth

While baking the squash, bake a couple of potatoes at the same time. When the potatoes are done, the squash will be too, and the combination is a real winner. It's healthful too, for the squash and its sauce replace butter and sour cream easily and deliciously.
Enjoy!

Easy Dates and Nuts

View of the Whole

*Delicious and easy don't always match up as well as they
do in this combination. If meditation—or quiet space—appeals to you,
give yourself that gift of the time you save cooking when you serve this dessert.*

1 cup pitted dates
2 cups walnuts
2 tsp. apple (or other fruit) juice

Chop pitted dates. Chop walnuts as finely as possible. Mix dates and walnuts with apple juice. Roll this "dough" into one-inch balls. Flatten slightly on an unbuttered cookie sheet. Bake at 325° for 15 minutes or until slightly browned.

Makes the easiest 30 cookies you ever baked!

Embracing Mother Earth

*If you're allergic to anything—besides dates and nuts—this
makes a great dessert for you. It feels special enough to be a treat,
not a penance for having an allergy. It feels special whether or not you're allergic,
so enjoy!*

Borscht Summer or Winter

View of the Whole

*The subtlety of blended flavors is known only to the cook.
Our awareness of the foods we eat is increased when we focus
on the ingredients that go into the dishes we prepare.
The same awareness is a key to understanding the subtlety
of our thought processes as well.*

4 cups vegetable stock or water
3 cups cabbage, chopped
2 medium beets, shredded
1 medium carrot, diced
1 tomato, chopped
2 Tbsp. lemon juice and pulp
1 Tbsp. Bragg's Liquid Aminos
2 Tbsp. tahini (ground sesame seeds)
½ cup yogurt
bay leaf

In a large cooking pot, combine stock with cabbage, beets, carrot and bay. Bring to a boil, cover, and simmer 30 minutes. Add tomato, lemon juice and liquid aminos, and cook 15 minutes longer. In a blender, put yogurt and tahini. Add half of the other mixture and blend well. Combine with remaining mixture and stir. Serve hot or cold.
Serves 6.

Embracing Mother Earth

*Cabbage and beets—mainstays of a winter harvest,
but also of early summer—create either a cool summer supper
or a hot winter dish. Either way, you can enjoy the fruits of the garden.
Enjoy!*

Applesauce Cake

View of the Whole

*Apples are a blessing when they fall freely from the tree and await your
pleasure. Bruised or nibbled on (from without or within), they still make great
applesauce. We can appreciate their wholeness—and our own—as we select the
edible parts and prepare the remainder to be composted back into the Earth.
We do well when we consider our own thoughts as carefully.*

¼ cup butter
⅓ cup honey
1 tsp. cinnamon
¼ tsp. cloves
½ tsp. nutmeg
1½ cups whole wheat flour
1 tsp. baking powder
1 tsp. baking soda
1 cup fresh applesauce
½ cup slivered almonds
½ cup raisins

Melt butter and honey together in the oven while it heats to 350°. Stir in
spices, then other dry ingredients. Add applesauce and mix vigorously for
3 minutes. Add nuts and/or raisins, if you choose. Spread in a 9" x 9" baking
pan and bake 30-35 minutes, or until it tests done.
Serves 9.

Embracing Mother Earth

*When the early apples fall, the weather is usually still hot.
Bake delectables like this in the late evening, so the house can
cool overnight. This saves energy—yours and the electricity.
Enjoy!*

Autumn

As I become
a part of the garden
breathing with the apple tree
listening to the pears ripen
opening petal after petal
of my being
I encompass
more
of the patterns of growth
the gentle guidance
that moves the seasons
and the sun
in their rounds
that are my rounds
that are eternity
viewed from the dewdrop
in its fullness
and my own

—h.k.

Celery and Apple Soup

View of the Whole

*A great way to celebrate the harvest season is to use nature's bounty in a
soup that can be served either hot or cold, depending on the day.
This one brings contented "m-m-m-m's" from eaters, and the cook
can be contented too, for the preparation is quick and easy.*

3 Tbsp. vegetable oil
2 large celery stalks, sliced
1 medium carrot, sliced
5 medium apples, unpeeled, cored & thinly sliced
1 tsp. Bragg's Liquid Aminos
1 cup vegetable stock or water
1 cup apple juice
1 cup milk
yogurt for garnish

Sauté celery and carrot in oil for 5 minutes. Add apples; increase heat and
cook 5-10 minutes, until apples are soft. Add liquids; when they boil, reduce
heat and simmer 5-10 minutes. Remove from heat and purée in blender in
small batches. Return to pan, adding milk if you want thinner soup. Warm
over low heat. Garnish soup bowls with yogurt. Serve hot or chilled.
Serves 6.

Embracing Mother Earth

*Apples are a mainstay in autumn, but do not often become a part of the main
meal as they do here. The slight sweetness of fresh, ripe apples makes this soup
almost delicious enough to serve as a dessert, or at least as a light beginning
to a heavier meal. It also can stand alone, perhaps as a lunch entrée.
However you choose to serve it, eat it with love and with remembrance
for the goodness of our planet who provides its sweetness.*
Enjoy!

Orange Rice Pudding

View of the Whole

Grains of rice meld when sweetened and simmered together.
Just so, our thoughts become the glue that holds together a world that can
seem shattered if we notice only the small grains and not its wholeness.

4 cups milk, scalded
1 cup brown rice
peel of one unsprayed orange
¼ cup honey
½ tsp. sea salt
2 Tbsp. cornstarch
½ tsp. vanilla
1 tsp. cinnamon

Heat milk in the top of a double boiler until bubbles form around the edge.
Add rice, orange peel, honey and salt. Heat over boiling water 1½ hours or
until soft, stirring occasionally. Remove orange peel. Mix cornstarch with ¼
cup cold water and add to rice mixture, stirring (still over boiling water) until
thickened, another 5-10 minutes. Remove from heat; add vanilla. Serve
warm or cool, topped with cinnamon.
Serves 8.

Embracing Mother Earth

Save orange peels when using unsprayed oranges. They come in handy for
recipes like this, or to grate to freshen a favorite cookie recipe or main dish.
You can freeze the peels if you don't use them often; the frozen peels are
easier to grate, in fact. Or keep them refrigerated if you like them often.
Enjoy!

Eggplant Ricotta

View of the Whole

*Shiny purple eggplants appear on harvest-laden vegetable
stands now, bringing forth another dimension of autumn cookery. As the
temperatures cool, baking dinner seems once again appropriate, and this twice
baked version is especially delicious. Heat purifies not only our food, but
our thoughts, when we risk paying attention to those burning inside our heads
and act on them. We too move into another dimension in the process.*

**3 medium eggplants
¾ cup wheat germ
2 green peppers, chopped
fresh oregano and basil, chopped
1 lb. mozzarella, grated
2 lbs. ricotta cheese
2 large tomatoes, sliced
Bragg's Liquid Aminos and pepper to taste**

Slice the eggplants into rounds. Bake at 350° for 15 minutes (or until
tender) on a buttered tray. Sprinkle the eggplant with wheat germ.

Meanwhile, sauté the pepper and herbs in 2 Tbsp. butter until soft. Combine
with the cheeses. Spread cheese mixture on half the eggplant. Top with
tomatoes, then another layer of eggplant and tomato. Bake covered for 35
minutes; uncover for the last 5 minutes.
Serves 6.

Embracing Mother Earth

*Fresh herbs enhance the cooking process, like seasoning our world
with spicy new thoughts. They're so easy to grow and take so little space
they become an important part of who we are as food preparers. Besides,
it's fun to go outside and snip a bit of basil just before cooking dinner.*
Enjoy!

Finnish Whipped Fruit Soup

View of the Whole

*The time it takes to bring this soup to its fluffy consistency
is time well spent pondering ways in which our thoughts
also change into more effective actions when enthusiastic
attention is applied to them.*

3 cups fruit juice
¼ cup honey, or less to taste
½ cup raw farina, noninstant
dash each of cinnamon and nutmeg
1 cup yogurt
1 cup fresh fruit (sliced peaches, grated apples, berries)
juice of ½ lemon

Heat juice and honey to boiling. Sprinkle in farina and spices; cook, stirring
constantly, until thick and smooth, 8-10 minutes. Pour into large bowl and
whip with wire whisk until light and fluffy, about 15 minutes. (It will change
color and consistency by then.) Fold in yogurt and fruit, on which lemon juice
has been sprinkled so it will not turn dark. Chill.
Serves 6-8.

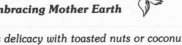

Embracing Mother Earth

*You can top this delicacy with toasted nuts or coconut,
or grated orange or lemon peel. You can mix several fruits together.
You can do as you choose, depending on the season, your garden's
bounty (or your friends'), and you and your guests' inclinations.
Mostly, enjoy!*

Rice and Pears

View of the Whole

*This combination is not something you'd think of every day, if at all.
It can help us move beyond "old patterns" and into new ways of relating with
our food. Sometimes it's fun to select new combinations simply for that purpose.
Try combining new thoughts in the same way, just to see what happens.*

**1 cup brown rice
2¼ cups vegetable stock or water
2 cups shredded cabbage
1 cup thinly sliced carrots
1 cup thinly sliced celery
1 Tbsp. unrefined vegetable oil
2 pears, chopped
2 Tbsp. chopped parsley
2 Tbsp. dill weed
1 tsp. cinnamon
½ tsp. dry mustard**

Boil rice in vegetable stock 45 minutes without removing cover. Remove from heat and let it stand 10 minutes before peeking. Stir with fork to fluff it up.

Meanwhile, sauté cabbage, carrots and celery in oil until slightly tender, adding a few tablespoons of stock if needed so vegetables don't stick to the pan. Stir in other ingredients, then add rice and mix together.
Serves 6.

Embracing Mother Earth

*This is truly a meal-in-one. Those who prefer to separate
the eating of vegetables and fruits can look to other recipes.
Each of us needs simply to listen to our own body in this regard—as
in all others. If this delightful dish sounds intriguing, try it.
In that case, enjoy!*

Quasi-choc Pudding

View of the Whole

Sometimes we can fool ourselves into new patterns by suggesting old favorites that have a new ingredient, whether it be food or thoughts. It's a fun game and worth a chuckle when you know you're doing it to feel better.

2 cups tofu, cut in pieces
2 bananas
2 Tbsp. peanut butter
2 Tbsp. carob powder
6 Tbsp. honey
¼ cup sunflower seeds
¼ cup grated coconut

Combine first five ingredients in a bowl and blend in small batches in a blender until smooth. Mix in sunflower seeds and chill in refrigerator until serving time.

Meanwhile, in a dry skillet toast grated coconut just until it starts to brown and smell good. Spoon pudding into serving dishes and top with coconut. *Serves 4.*

Embracing Mother Earth

From the oohs and ahhs heard the first time this was served, it indeed hit the right spot. It's a good, healthy alternative to chocolate whipped cream that you can really enjoy and feel good about.
Enjoy!

Brigands' Pasta Adapted

View of the Whole

Recipes from magazines, like any good book (according to Emerson), serve only to whet your own appetite to create. This pasta sauce is no exception, but the basics described here also serve well on their own.

1½ lbs. broccoli, trimmed
½ cup vegetable oil
2 lbs. tomatoes, chopped
Bragg's Liquid Aminos, to taste
½ cup raisins
½ cup walnuts or pine nuts
1 lb. pasta
½ cup chopped parsley

Cut broccoli into small flowerets and steam just until tender, 5-7 minutes; then drain. Put oil in large, heavy skillet; add tomatoes and liquid aminos, and cook 10 minutes over medium high heat, stirring occasionally. Add raisins and nuts, and cook 5 minutes longer. Add broccoli and mix until heated through.

Meanwhile, cook pasta in separate pan until just tender. Drain well. Mix in sauce and parsley.
Serves 4.

Embracing Mother Earth

Save those broccoli stems! Steam them when you're done cooking the flowerets, and refrigerate to use in another soup later. Roma (or small sauce) tomatoes, if in season, are great in this sauce. You can add herbs to taste; basil and rosemary work well. Enjoy!

Louisa May Alcott's Apple Slump

View of the Whole

*Autumn continues the apple harvest, and different ways to serve apples
are always welcome. Yet in each way, we become more aware
of nature's bounty and our own good fortune to enjoy it.*

6 cups cooked, sliced apples
¼ cup apple juice
¼ cup honey
1 tsp. cinnamon
½ tsp. nutmeg
1½ cups whole wheat pastry flour
1½ tsp. baking powder
2 Tbsp. softened butter
¾ cup milk
½ cup raisins

Combine apples and juice with ¼ cup honey, cinnamon, and nutmeg in
large heavy skillet (with lid). Cook over medium heat until mixture boils. In
a bowl, mix the flour and baking powder well. Cut in butter with a fork. Add
milk and raisins, and mix until blended. Spoon on top of simmering apple
mixture. Cover and simmer 15-20 minutes or until dumplings are done.
Serves 6-8.

Embracing Mother Earth

This recipe is a variation on the one in Little Women. *It was
included in* Apple Encore, *a book produced by Harriet Kimbro
(me in a previous incarnation). Now it's been modified to reduce the
sweetening and switch it from sugar to honey. This can be done with
any recipe, in fact. Usually, one-half the amount of honey replaces
all the sugar. In this one, you can do without any sweetening,
if you prefer, or if your apples are especially sweet.
It always pays to experiment to suit your own taste.
Enjoy!*

Roasted Pumpkin Seeds

View of the Whole

*Pumpkin purée is great, but don't forget the seeds! The
fruits of our labors also produce the seeds that create our future.*

Cut open a fresh pumpkin and scoop out the seeds, removing as much of
the fiber as possible. Put seeds in a single layer on a large cookie sheet and
sprinkle with 1-2 Tbsp. unrefined vegetable oil and 2 tsp. liquid aminos.
Bake at 300° until crisp, about 30-40 minutes. Eat while hot! Yes, you can
eat the whole seed.

Gingered Pumpkin Soup

1 Tbsp. butter
1 Tbsp. shredded fresh ginger
2 cups cooked pumpkin or winter squash
4 cups vegetable stock or water
1 Tbsp. Bragg's Liquid Aminos
½ cup milk
¼ cup dry milk (optional)

Heat butter in a large pot and sauté ginger to soften. Put the pumpkin and
part of the liquid in a blender and blend until smooth. Add butter and ginger,
plus other ingredients. Heat, but do not boil. Serve with fresh bread and a
salad.

Serves 6.

To cook pumpkin: Depending on its size, cut the pumpkin into quarters
or slices. Put on a large baking sheet and bake at 350° for 30 minutes or
until a fork pierces the pulp (not skin) easily. Peel or cut away the outer skin,
and cut pulp into cubes.

Embracing Mother Earth

*It's definitely worthwhile to begin this meal with a fresh pumpkin or squash,
if for no other reason than having the seeds to roast. And it's almost worth
taking a portion of your land to grow a pumpkin for yourself.
However, the energy in doing so, and in watering the vine,
may seem inefficient to you. Wherever you get the pumpkin,
enjoy!*

Natural Autumn Grape Delight

View of the Whole

*Concord grapes and their cousins hang heavy from the vines
in autumn, their scent filling the air. We can almost watch the fruit develop,
just as our ripening thoughts scent the air through our words and actions.*

**3 lbs. fresh Concord grapes
2 Tbsp. agar*
1 cup whipping cream**

Wash and stem fresh grapes. Heat to boiling and simmer 5 minutes. Pour through sieve to extract the juice and pulp. Sprinkle agar on juice and pulp. Let it sit for 5 minutes; then boil 2-3 minutes until agar melts. Let the liquid stand until it reaches room temperature. Whip cream till firm and fold into grape mixture. Refrigerate until serving time, at least several hours if you want it thick.
Serves 8.

*Agar is made from seaweed, whereas gelatin is made from calves' hooves. If you're conscious of animal products, be aware of any food thickened with gelatin. Agar is used a bit differently, but provides a delightful alternative that tastes good and feels much more in tune with nature. It comes in different strengths, so check the package label for proportions and vary liquids accordingly.

Options:
Fresh berries and any other fruit you enjoy works just as well. Vary spices to suit your taste. General proportions are 2 cups of fruit juice to 1 Tbsp. of agar. You can add 1-2 cups of chopped fruit and ¼ cup each of fresh lemon juice and honey, and omit the whipping cream if you prefer. One good variation is Bosc pears, a bit of minced candied ginger, and a dash of ground ginger and allspice. Unlike gelatin, agar will thicken raw pineapple.

Embracing Mother Earth

*Take advantage of this way to enjoy fresh fruit
especially when you have access to picking it fresh. What could be simpler
than fruit juice and whipped cream? The simplicity, both of ingredients and
preparation—with or without the cream—give this recipe an A+.
Enjoy!*

Eggplant Enchiladas

View of the Whole

A new twist on an old favorite provides a spicy flavor, healthfully. The unusual combination of flavors provides inspiration to combine our usual ways of doing things into new ways—a good process to ponder while toasting the tortillas.

6 cups cubed eggplant (2 small eggplants)
2 green or red sweet peppers, chopped
3 Tbsp. unrefined vegetable oil
1 tsp. Bragg's Liquid Aminos
1 tsp. cumin
1 cup slivered, toasted almonds
freshly ground black pepper
1 cup grated jack cheese
12 whole wheat tortillas

Sauté eggplant and peppers in oil, with liquid aminos and cumin. Cook until eggplant is soft, about 10 minutes. Meanwhile, toast almonds in a dry skillet over moderate heat, stirring until slightly brown. (Watch them carefully so they don't burn.) Add almonds and pepper to eggplant and cook another 5 minutes, stirring frequently. (This cooks down quite a bit, so be sure you have more than enough for the appetites you're serving.) Remove from heat and add cheese, mixing in well.

Warm tortillas one at a time in a large dry skillet over high heat, about 30 seconds on a side. Keep warm in a towel until all are done. You may serve this dish by spreading the eggplant sauce on the tortillas and topping with cheese. Or you may put ¼ cup of sauce (with cheese mixed in) on each tortilla, roll up, and place gently in a baking pan. Pour remaining sauce on top and bake at 350° for 20 minutes.
Serves 4-6.

Embracing Mother Earth

The crunch of almonds is a surprise in this dish.
Proportions of ingredients may be varied to taste.
This autumn time of year, thin sweet Italian peppers
are a wonderful addition, or tomatillos, little green Mexican
tomatoes, might also be a good addition. Whatever you add,
enjoy!

Applesauce Cookies

View of the Whole

*This is like a baked breakfast treat! Sweets can serve as reminders
to keep our thoughts and words sweet. The better to whisper sweet words
to our Mother Earth for providing all we need.*

¾ cup unrefined vegetable oil
¼ cup honey
½ cup chopped nuts or
 sunflower seeds (or combination)
½ tsp. sea salt
1 cup thick applesauce
1 tsp. vanilla
4 cups rolled oats
½ cup raisins or chopped dates
1 tsp. cinnamon
¼ cup yogurt, or as needed

Mix together all ingredients, adding yogurt as needed to hold ingredients
together. Drop by small spoonfuls on a buttered cookie sheet. Bake at 375°
for 20-25 minutes or until browned. Cool on the cookie sheet.
Makes 5 dozen.

Embracing Mother Earth

*When traveling, it helps to carry homemade goodies to snack on,
being careful about the ingredients used so they will keep well.
These cookies work well as treats for the road.*
Enjoy!

Double Red Soup Surprise

View of the Whole

*Nobody ever said it couldn't be done. This surprising
combination was accidental—at first. It tasted so good it became an instant
successful addition to autumn's repertoire. Don't knock it until you try it! We
sometimes surprise ourselves with an unexpected thought. When we learn to
trust our intuition more and listen to that surprise, we increase our own
appreciation of instant success in our lives.*

2-3 lbs. fresh beets
½ lb. fresh Concord-type grapes
yogurt for topping
fortitude and love of adventure

Wash beets, cut in pieces, and steam them until almost tender, about 15
minutes. Cut a few chunks into bite-size pieces; run the rest through the
blender with just enough juice to purée them. Add bite-size pieces back in
and set mixture aside.

Stem grapes and simmer in a little water for 10 minutes. Run them through
a sieve to extract the juice. To 4 cups of beets add 1 cup of grape juice. Heat
thoroughly and serve topped with yogurt (if desired).
Serves 4-5, with baked potatoes to make a meal.

Baked Potatoes: For each person, select a firm thick potato. Scrub well
and coat lightly with unrefined vegetable oil. Prick several times with a fork.
Bake at 400° for 45-60 minutes, depending on size of potatoes, or until they
give slightly when you squeeze them. Delicious with butter and yogurt and
a sprinkling of fresh ground black pepper. Because of their high nutritional
value, potatoes make a meal in themselves with a fresh vegetable or soup.

Embracing Mother Earth

*Only because the containers looked alike
did I happen to add leftover grape juice
to some cooked beets. You can do it on purpose,
as I did afterward. Creating meals is a daily adventure.
Enjoy!*

Chunky Pumpkin Pie

View of the Whole

We are so conditioned to pumpkin purée that we've forgotten what pumpkin pieces are like. Their texture is crunchy and seems unusual, though familiar. It does take a bit of time to chop raw pumpkin finely, but it's worth the effort for this eating adventure. This pie is a good reminder that there's always another way to view life if we simply take time to experience it anew.

6 cups raw pumpkin (2-3 lb.)
½ cup honey
1 tsp. cinnamon
5 Tbsp. whole wheat pastry flour
2 Tbsp. butter

Peel and core the pumpkin; cut into ½ " cubes. Mix with honey, cinnamon and flour; pour mixture into prepared pie shell. Dot with butter. Cover with top crust. Bake at 350° for one hour or until top crust is lightly browned.

Whole Wheat Pastry

3 cups whole wheat pastry flour
½ tsp. sea salt
½ cup melted butter or
unrefined vegetable oil
½-¾ cup ice water

Combine flour and salt. Add butter while stirring with a fork. Add ice water 1 Tbsp. at a time until dough forms a ball that barely holds together. Divide in half and roll each piece out between layers of wax paper. For a two-crust pie like this one, slit top crust for steam holes before putting on top of filling.

Embracing Mother Earth

This crust is also good in a single pie shell. You can freeze the dough, so make extra while you're at it. To use frozen dough, warm it to room temperature and then roll it out. However you use it, enjoy!

Pilgrims' Delight

View of the Whole

As the hard-skinned winter squash come in, so do the delightfully curious gourds. Harvest is truly here! And we can enjoy the delights of the many curious varieties of squash now too, from turbans to butternut to delicata. So too do we harvest the many curious delights of our own thoughts.

3 cups winter squash, peeled and cubed (about 1 lb.)
3 cups cabbage, coarsely chopped (about ½ lb.)
1 cup uncooked bulgur
1 cup dried yellow split peas
1 stalk of fennel root, sliced, or 1 tsp. dill weed
bell pepper, chopped (or a hot pepper if you prefer)
2 Tbsp. Bragg's Liquid Aminos
6 cups vegetable stock or water

In a large pot, combine all ingredients. Bring to a boil and simmer until peas are tender, about 1¼ hours. You can add herbs to taste, but it's good simply like this so you can enjoy each flavor by itself.
Serves 6-8.

Embracing Mother Earth

Any of the winter squash will work, but you can make the process easier on yourself by selecting one that's easy to peel, like delicata or butternut. Any way you make this it's a hefty dinner dish, fit for the Pilgrims who must have feasted on the likes of this.
Enjoy!

Easy Apples

View of the Whole

*Just as we balance our intense and quiet times in life,
it's important to balance heavier meals
with a light dessert. This is about as light
and as easy as they come.*

**4 apples
1 Tbsp. honey
1 Tbsp. lemon juice
½ cup chopped dates
1 cup yogurt
¼ cup slivered almonds**

Cut apples in quarters and core them. Shred (including skins, unless too tough to grate) into a large bowl. Sprinkle with honey and lemon juice. Stir in dates, yogurt and almonds.
Serves 4.

Embracing Mother Earth

Peeled apples darken quickly in the open air. If you're shredding more than 4 apples, sprinkle lemon juice on the gratings as you go so they won't turn dark. You can vary the amount of dates to suit your taste and to complement the tartness of the apples you choose. Raisins would substitute if dates aren't available or handy, as would nuts other than almonds. But dates have properties that are good to take in occasionally, and almonds are the highest in nutritional value of the common nuts. However you vary this recipe, enjoy!

One More Pasta

View of the Whole

Is there ever an end to new ways to sauce pasta? Here's one that invented itself—as many do—from ingredients available in the refrigerator. It's a good time to remember that our thoughts combine themselves in new ways when we're aware that they are available for that pleasure. Take time to listen to your own inner self. You're worth it.

½ lb. pasta
1 large fresh tomato
3 chopped tomatillos
 (small green Mexican tomatoe)
2 Tbsp. unrefined vegetable oil
1 cup sprouted garbanzo beans
2 medium zucchini
1 tsp. basil

Prepare your favorite pasta (whole wheat is good). Meanwhile in a heavy skillet, combine the other ingredients. Simmer 15 minutes. Pour sauce over hot pasta.
Serves 2, and the leftovers are even tastier after the flavors blend awhile.

Embracing Mother Earth

Be sure to freeze some basil cubes to freshen winter meals. Simply put fresh basil (stems, leaves and all) in the blender with a small amount of vegetable stock or water, just enough so the basil will purée. Pour the purée into an ice cube tray and freeze .When frozen, remove cubes and seal them in containers or bags. When you make winter soups, add a cube or two and enjoy!

Everyday Cookies

View of the Whole

*In the 1940s, when this recipe was published in a honey cookbook,
the cookies bore this name. It's been a long time since we had such
treats "every day". Change is the nature of life—and of cookies.
We can appreciate it more when we glance back from time to time
and see how far we've come, and look ahead knowing we have the choice
now of how to create what's coming. How about cookies every day?*

½ cup butter
½ cup honey
¾ cup whole wheat pastry flour
½ tsp. baking powder
½ tsp. baking soda
1 cup oats
1 cup shredded coconut
1 tsp. vanilla
½ cup chopped nuts and sunflower seeds

Melt butter and honey in the oven while it heats to 350°. Meanwhile, mix
flour, baking powder and baking soda; combine with butter and honey. Stir
in oats, coconut and vanilla. Add nuts. Drop by small spoonfuls on buttered
baking sheet. Bake for 12-15 minutes, until light brown around the edges.
Makes 3-4 dozen.

Embracing Mother Earth

*A good technique to use to save energy is to warm or melt ingredients like butter
and honey in the oven while it's preheating to baking temperature. And be
prepared; cookies like these will encourage your eaters to want them "every day."
Enjoy!*

Lima-Corn Chowder

View of the Whole

The delicate combination of ingredients brings out the best on a crisp autumn day. The crunch of the corn adds good texture, and the cheese tops the flavoring. We do well to flavor our inner processes with such attention to their delicate combinations, and to top them with the spice of risking a new way of seeing the moment.

½ lb. dried lima beans*
¼ cup butter
2 ribs celery, chopped
½ tsp. sea salt
¼ cup flour

freshly ground black pepper
2 cups milk
2 cups tomatoes, chopped
2 cups corn kernels
¼ lb. sharp cheddar cheese, grated

Rinse limas and cover with water; soak 6 hours or overnight. Drain and cover with 6 cups vegetable stock or fresh water. Simmer 1 hour *uncovered*. Sauté celery in butter. Add flour, salt and pepper; stir well. Add milk and bring just to a boil (but don't boil). Add beans, their liquid and other ingredients. Heat just to boiling.
Serves 8.

* *Lima beans, unlike other beans, contain enough potentially toxic cyanide compounds that they require special cooking attention. Boil in an uncovered pot and the cyanide gas will escape in the steam. Prepare all lima beans—fresh, dried, or sprouted—this way.*

Options:
Instead of celery, you can substitute any handy green stems, such as bok choy or chard. Add some of the leafy part and the soup becomes a meal in itself. You can also serve it with a green pepper, zucchini, tomato (if available) and carrots, dressed with unrefined vegetable oil and rice vinegar in 2 to 1 proportions.

Embracing Mother Earth

If it's too late in the season for fresh vegetables and you don't have home-frozen ones, you can use canned vegetables in soup. But do so as a last resort; the high temperatures destroy enzymes so canned food has minimal nutritional value. Be aware of this difference and, whenever possible, choose raw unprocessed foods. Enjoy!

Brown Soda Bread

View of the Whole

*Kneading bread provides a few minutes to focus thoughts on the project
at hand and to consciously add positive energy to the food we prepare.
That habit can then help us on more subtle levels when we "need" it as well.*

2 cups whole wheat flour
2 cups unbleached white flour
1 tsp. baking powder
½ tsp. sea salt
¾ cup or more buttermilk or sour milk

Flour a baking sheet. Combine dry ingredients. Add milk until soft dough forms. Knead 12 times (or gently until smooth). Form on the baking sheet into a 1" high, 8" round. Bake at 350° until brown and it sounds hollow, approximately 50-60 minutes. Cool 15 minutes and serve with honey or fresh jam for a delicious dessert.
Serves 6-8.

Embracing Mother Earth

*If you don't have buttermilk on hand, you can create your own
good-tasting sour milk for recipes like this simply by adding 2 Tbsp. lemon
juice to 1 cup fresh milk. Let it stand 5 minutes and it's ready to use.
Enjoy!*

Annette's Vegetable Chili

View of the Whole

*The satisfaction that comes from stirring the pot makes the
effort of cooking this well worthwhile. It's like stirring ideas in one's mind
when we give ourselves permission to daydream or envision the best world we can.*

1 cup dry garbanzo beans
1 cup dry pinto beans
⅓ cup unrefined vegetable oil
2 medium zucchini, chopped
2 large sweet red peppers, chopped
1-28 oz. can plum tomatoes
1½ lbs. fresh plum tomatoes, chopped
1 Tbsp. chili powder
1 Tbsp. each dried basil and oregano
1 Tbsp. ground cumin
2 tsp. fresh ground black pepper
1 Tbsp. Bragg's Liquid Aminos
½ cup chopped parsley
1 tsp. fennel seeds
½ cup fresh dill weed or 1 tsp. dried dill
2 Tbsp. fresh lemon juice

In separate containers, cover the beans with 2" of water to soak overnight.
Drain; cover garbanzos again with vegetable stock or water and cook over
low heat for one hour. Add pintos and cook an additional 1½ hours, until
beans are tender.

Meanwhile, heat oil in a large skillet. Add chopped zucchini and peppers,
and cook 5 minutes or until slightly soft. Add tomatoes and herbs (except
dill and lemon juice); cook uncovered for 30 minutes, stirring often. Add dill
and lemon juice; cook 15 minutes longer. Combine with cooked beans.
Serves 4-6.

Embracing Mother Earth

*You can add sprouted beans to this soup
to add the subtle nutrition of their life force to your meal.
It's like gardening, one step removed, as you plant the sprouted beans
in the soil of your cooking water and watch them bear the fruit of your dinner.
Enjoy!*

Easy Applesauce

View of the Whole

*One of the simplest ways to eat apples, other than chomping them whole, is this
version of uncooked sauce. It's a nice contrast to the main course as well. And
the health benefits of combining raw and cooked foods is an advantage we could
do well to learn more about. This dish offers a good chance to focus on the
benefits of our own raw thoughts, well blended and spiced, to add the finishing
touch to an otherwise incomplete meal within our spirit as well as within our body.*

4 unpeeled apples, chopped
1 tsp. cinnamon
2 tsp. lemon juice
honey to taste (optional)

Blend apples until smooth. Stir in cinnamon and lemon juice (to keep them
from turning dark). If apples are too tart, a small amount of honey may also
be added.

*Serves 2-3. (If your blender container has measurements, figure ½ cup per
person.)*

Embracing Mother Earth

*When apples come in, it's time to get out all the available recipes to try.
This one's particularly good for windfalls. You can cut out bad spots
and toss the good chunks into the blender. The pectin in the apples aids digestion,
a good point to remember in order to balance meals that can use that help.*
Enjoy!

Stuffed Peppers

View of the Whole

*Pungent aromas of autumn and cool days bring forth the
tastes of oven-baked main dishes. Making use of autumn crispness to heat the
house with the smells of dinner cooking enhances the appetites of all who
enjoy the process. Remembering this is as important as the ingredients you
use. Preparing meals then becomes an inner process as well as one on the
stove, and the cook also enjoys it more as a result.*

2 large green peppers
2 Tbsp. unrefined vegetable oil
¼ cup celery, diced
¼ cup chopped walnuts
1 carrot, grated
1 cup cooked brown rice
⅓ cup grated cheddar cheese
2 tsp. Bragg's Liquid Aminos

Cut a thin slice from the top of the peppers. Scoop out seeds and core. Chop
the tops and sauté in oil in a skillet with the celery, walnuts and carrot.
Mix in rice, ¼ cup cheddar and liquid aminos. Use mixture to stuff in
peppers. Set in a baking dish with ½ " of hot water in the bottom. Sprinkle
tops of peppers with remaining grated cheese. Bake at 375° for 35-45
minutes.
Serves 2.

Options:
When available, fresh mushrooms chopped into the mixture are a good addition.
Lentils cooked with the rice add a subtle flavor that enhances all the ingredients.

Embracing Mother Earth

*While peppers are plentiful, this is a good choice for an autumn dinner.
It makes use of warm sustenance for those cooling days that foretell what's
to come. Cooking the rice in vegetable stock instead of water not only
improves its nutritional value, but adds subtle flavor to the stuffing as well.
Enjoy!*

Cape Cod Oatmeal Cookies

View of the Whole

"The Vermomt Beekeeper's Cookbook" turned up the recipe from which this treasure evolved. Whether you're on the Cape or in a city, oatmeal cookies offer your body, and those of your friends, a treat to be enjoyed often. So many people think cookies are for holidays or for children, but we can all celebrate ourselves any time with little effort.

½ cup butter
½ cup honey
1 Tbsp. molasses
½ tsp. baking soda
1 tsp. cinnamon
1½ cups whole wheat pastry flour
1¾ cups oats
2 Tbsp. yogurt
1 cup raisins, currants, nuts, sunflower seeds
(or combination)

Melt butter with honey and molasses in the oven as you heat it to 350°. Stir together dry ingredients; add all the wet ones. Bake on buttered cookie sheet for 12-14 minutes, until lightly browned.
Makes 4 dozen, enough to satisfy your palette for awhile and come back to make more.

Embracing Mother Earth

Oats are beneficial to lower cholesterol, but they're also hearty fare simply to enjoy. Mixing nuts and seeds improves the protein value of any food you concoct. Yogurt is an easy substitute for eggs. You can vary the amount and type of molasses to suit your taste. It, and the raisins, are very high in iron, another benefit of these delicious treats.
Enjoy!

Creamy Corn and Zucchini

View of the Whole

*Amazingly quick and easy, this is a winner for sure!
And it embraces the last of summer's corn and the final squash
as frost takes over the garden. Amazing too is the speed with which
our thoughts can change seasons. When we observe the process,
we learn more about ourselves more quickly, and we can
embrace all of who we are.*

1 small sweet red pepper (optional)
2 Tbsp. unrefined vegetable oil
2 medium zucchini
1 Tbsp. vegetable stock or water
1 cup (or more) corn kernels, cooked
½ cup cottage cheese
2 tsp. Bragg's Liquid Aminos
fresh black pepper
¼ cup mashed tofu

Sauté pepper (if used) in oil; add zucchini and 1 Tbsp. vegetable stock or water. Cover and steam 5 minutes. Add corn, mix, and steam 2 minutes longer. Mix other ingredients and pour over hot vegetables. Stir to combine, cover and cook 2 minutes longer to heat through.
Serves 2.

Embracing Mother Earth

*Satisfies the palate as well as the appetite,
a joy to prepare, to serve, and to eat.
Enjoy!*

Johnny Appleseed Cake

View of the Whole

Nature's bounty is so magnificent at this autumn time of year that it's easy to find ways to appreciate her. This cake is certainly one of them, and teaches us to appreciate the bounty of our own existence in every season, but especially in this moment. Then we can plant the seeds of that joy in all that we do.

**2 cups whole wheat pastry flour
1 tsp. cinnamon
½ tsp. ground nutmeg
¼ tsp. ground cloves
2 tsp. baking soda
1 cup raisins
1 cup coarsely chopped walnuts
½ cup butter
½ cup honey
3 Tbsp. molasses
1½ cups applesauce**

Mix together the dry ingredients, raisins, and walnuts in a large bowl. Melt the butter in the oven while it heats; mix with honey, molasses and applesauce. Add wet to dry ingredients and mix thoroughly. Pour batter into a well buttered 9" x 9" pan. Bake at 325° for 40-60 minutes, or until a toothpick inserted in the center comes out clean.
Serves 8.

Options:
May be topped with Cream Cheese Frosting (pg. 123) if you like to gild the lily but it's great by itself too.

Embracing Mother Earth

Apples in abundance—what a treat! If they fall faster than you can eat them, make applesauce and freeze it. Simply cut up the apples, skin and all, and simmer in a small amout of apple juice or water for 15-20 minutes until tender. Purée in the blender and freeze. Then you can make this delicious cake any time.
Enjoy!

Zucchini–Again

View of the Whole

*Harvest time creates new spaces in the kitchen—not
in physical space, but in ways to view the coming together
of the seasons and the melding of the flavors of friends,
events, processes, into the whole that is the soup of life.*

**1 cup brown rice, cooked
4 small zucchini, sliced and
  steamed lightly
2 fresh tomatoes, cubed
1 cup shredded cheddar cheese
1 tsp. dried basil (or fresh, to
  taste)
1 tsp. Bragg's Liquid Aminos
dry bread crumbs, or
  crumbled corn chips**

Put cooked rice in the bottom of a buttered baking dish. Add the steamed
zucchini, then fresh tomatoes. Top with cheese and basil. Sprinkle with liquid
aminos and top with chips. Bake at 350° for 15 minutes or until cheese
is melted and bubbly.
Serves 4-6.

Embracing Mother Earth

*Adding a fresh tomato (not steamed like the zucchini) imparts
a fresh flavor to any dish. It's a good way to freshen up a winter dish,
when tamatoes are costly but one is affordable. Different cheeses may be
used with this; cheddar, especially sharp, is more flavorful than some
and thus a personal favorite of mine. Other herbs may be added, but
the simplicity of using just basil has a special quality.
Enjoy!*

Oats and More Oats Cookies

View of the Whole

*Avoiding both wheat and eggs in cookies isn't always easy; this does
both, and does it well. With a little effort, we can meet our own goals,
whether they be of diet, of thought, or of other actions. It simply
requires remembering in a positive way why we're making the effort
(a word that simply means "to make strong").*

⅓ cup unrefined vegetable oil
⅓ cup butter
¼ cup honey
¼ cup molasses
3½ cups oats
1 tsp. vanilla
1 tsp. cinnamon
pinch of salt
⅓ cup raisins

Cream oil, butter, honey and molasses until pale, about 3 minutes. At 100
strokes per minute, this is almost a thousand, a good time to remember the
thousand cranes that symbolize peace and health in the Japanese children's
story of Sadako.

Grind 2 cups of the oats in a blender. Combine ground oats, vanilla,
cinnamon and salt into a creamed mixture. Then add other oats and raisins.
Drop by small spoonfuls onto a cookie sheet. Flatten with a moistened
finger. Bake at 350° for about 12 minutes, or until lightly browned on the
bottom.
Makes 3 dozen cookies.

Embracing Mother Earth

*If you measure the oil first, it slicks the container
so it's then easy to measure honey and molasses in the same one.
Oats, a mainstay of the cookie-maker, come on strong
in these cookies that depend entirely on oats to hold them together.
Enjoy!*

Garbanzo Stew Anew

View of the Whole

*Similar in flavor to minestrone, this hefty stew serves as a main dinner dish
on cool rainy nights. Mingling flavors, mingling thoughts, we stir the ingredients
of our next meal—inner or outer. Native Americans stir clockwise, a
contemplative, purposeful motion in harmony with nature.
We can stir this way—inner or outer—as well.*

½ cup unrefined vegetable oil
5 cups cooked garbanzo beans
 (2 cups dry)
1 cup chopped parsley
2-3 tomatoes, chopped, or
 1 cup canned tomato purée
1 Tbsp. rosemary, crumbled
2 stalks celery, chopped
1 green pepper, chopped
4 cups vegetable stock or water
1 Tbsp. Bragg's Liquid Aminos
1 cup whole wheat macaroni, cooked
1 tsp. pepper (or to taste)
grated fresh cheese, like mozzarella

In a large pan, combine all ingredients except macaroni, pepper and cheese.
Simmer, covered, about 30 minutes, stirring occasionally. Meanwhile, cook
macaroni; drain and set aside. When sauce is well blended, add pepper and
macaroni and simmer 5-10 minutes, covered.
Serve with grated cheese, to 4.

Options:
Other beans, like adzukis, may be included with the garbanzos.

Embracing Mother Earth

*The parts of the vegetables that don't go into the stew begin the
collection to simmer later in water to create the next batch of vegetable
stock. Recycling isn't limited to cans and bottles. After having been cooked for the
stock, the stems and stalks compost more quickly,
helping the worms grow fat and your soil healthier. Everyone gains.
Enjoy!*

Favorite Poppyseed Cookies

View of the Whole

*We are indeed fortunate to have access to ingredients like
poppyseeds to bring elemental seeds into our physical diet,
just as we use the seeds of thoughts to make whole our inner life.*

½ cup milk
⅔ cup poppyseeds
½ cup raisins
¾ cup whole wheat pastry flour
½ cup unbleached white flour*
1 tsp. baking powder
½ cup butter
⅓ cup honey
½ tsp. vanilla or lemon
 extract
grated orange or lemon peel
(optional)

In saucepan, heat milk almost to boiling. Remove from fire and add
poppyseeds and raisins. Stir and set aside. Mix dry ingredients together.
Cream butter until smooth, and add honey and extract. Add dry ingredients,
then fold in poppyseed mixture and peel (if used). Place in small spoonfuls
slightly apart on buttered cookie sheet. Bake 15 minutes at 350° until light
brown at the edges. They will crisp as they cool.
Makes 3-4 dozen.

Note: The mix of flours helps to hold the cookies together in this recipe.

Embracing Mother Earth

*No doubt there's some important mineral in poppyseeds,
for they come to mind periodically almost as a craving.
This is one of the greatest ways I've discovered to satisfy that.
Enjoy them with me!*

Winter

The sunflower
grows
sustained by the Earth
warmed by sunlight
nurtured by all who pass by
she forms the seeds
of her own future
and of those who feed on her
she blooms when it is time
and in every season
she trusts each moment
in itself
for she is
also
the sun
flowering

−h.k.

Tamale Pie

View of the Whole

*The spiritual significance of cornmeal is almost unknown
in Western culture today. To indigenous peoples, corn represents humanity
with each kernel a human being. As we cook with cornmeal today,
we can contemplate this, and gain both the serenity of focused endeavor
and the joy of another level of meaning to the foods we eat.*

**2 cups dry pinto or kidney beans
1 Tbsp. cumin
1¼ cups cornmeal
2½ cups vegetable stock or water
1 tsp. Bragg's Liquid Aminos
1 tsp. chili powder
herbs to taste: cumin, basil, oregano, dill, thyme
2 cups fresh seasonal vegetables, chopped
2 Tbsp. tomato paste
1 cup grated cheese**

Cover beans with water and soak overnight. Drain and cover with vegetable stock or fresh water. Add cumin and simmer 2¼ hours or until tender. Meanwhile, mix cornmeal, stock, liquid aminos and ½ tsp. chili powder in a saucepan over medium heat. Stir continuously until mixture thickens and all the liquid is absorbed (about 10-15 minutes). Press mixture into sides and bottom of a buttered 9" x 13" x 1½" deep baking dish, saving ¼ of the amount to drop or spread on top later.

In a separate pan, combine cooked beans (which can be mashed with a potato masher, leaving some whole) with other ingredients except cheese. Cook over medium heat until vegetables are almost cooked. Pour into baking pan and spread evenly. Sprinkle grated cheese on top and spoon on remaining cornmeal mixture. Bake at 350° for 25 minutes.
Serves 6-8.

Embracing Mother Earth

*Save energy by using glass or Corningware pans,
which require an oven temperature 25° lower than metal pans.
Enjoy!*

Fruit Tzimmis

View of the Whole

*When fresh-fruit season leaves, our taste for fruit doesn't.
Using dried fruits during the winter, simmering them as in this recipe,
we scent the house with summertime. Even as spring bushes already
have tiny buds, so too can we envision the future ahead of us,
simply by savoring desserts like this.*

**3 cups (1 lb.) dried fruits: apricots,
raisins, prunes, papaya (not dates or figs)
water to cover
2 carrots, grated
1 lemon or lime, thinly sliced
2 apples, grated
1 Tbsp. butter**

Soak dried fruit in water for one hour. Drain water and reserve. Combine
soaked fruit and remaining ingredients in a saucepan with ½ cup of the
soaking water. Bring to a boil; then simmer very slowly for one or two
hours, adding more of the soaking water as needed.
Serves 6.

Embracing Mother Earth

*You can be creative with the variety of fruits used, but if possible choose organically
grown ones. (Simmering concentrates chemicals and preservatives in what you eat.)
Using small amounts of several different fruits makes this dish all the more
interesting, and the flavors blend well with the long cooking. Carrots are a delightfully unexpected addition, as is the tart lemon. No wonder Russian cooks favor
these on long winter days.
Enjoy!*

Savory Vegetable Sauce

View of the Whole

*Two favorite staples of vegetarians, spaghetti and tofu,
combine into a savory whole. When we join the staples in our own inner menu,
we strengthen ourselves into a savory whole as well. The parts of this whole
can be used in many ways, just as our thoughts can, to further enhance our diet.*

5-6 cups vegetables, chopped
4 cups tomatoes, chopped
  or 36 oz. tomato paste
4-8 cups vegetable stock or
  water (lesser amount with
  chopped tomatoes)

½ cup Bragg's Liquid Aminos
4 Tbsp. oregano
2 bay leaves
⅓ cup honey
3 Tbsp. basil
¼ tsp. cayenne pepper

Simmer all ingredients over medium heat for an hour. Add more liquid if you like it thinner. Makes about 22 cups, enough for 16 servings over spaghetti or rice.

Options:
You can freeze some for later use as pizza sauce or with stuffed bell peppers. It's also good on Polenta Bake (pg. 98).

Savory Tofu

4 cups firm tofu
¼ cup Bragg's Liquid Aminos
1 Tbsp. chopped parsley
1 tsp. basil
1 tsp. fennel seed

Rinse and drain tofu; chop into bite-size cubes. Combine all ingredients and spread in a single layer on a lightly buttered cookie sheet. Bake at 350° for 45 minutes, stirring occasionally.
Serves 4-6, with Savory Vegetable Sauce over spaghetti.

Embracing Mother Earth

*The shredded vegetables in this sauce suit the most jaded taste. Anything goes.
Enjoy!*

Apricot-Orange Dream

View of the Whole

*After a spicy meal, or a hefty one, fruit dessert adds a light balance.
In the same way, we can consciously balance our thought processes between heavy-
going times and those more delicate sweet thoughts that lead us to daydreams. It's
about awareness and using what we have to better advantage.*

**½ lb. dried apricots
1 medium orange
¼ cup honey
¼ cup walnuts, chopped
1 cup cream, whipped
carob chips, for topping**

Cover apricots with cold water and soak for several hours, until soft; then
drain and save liquid. Chop entire orange, including rind, in a blender. Add
orange and honey to apricots, with enough apricot soaking liquid to keep
them from sticking to the pot. Cook mixture over very low heat until tender
and most of the liquid is absorbed, about 10-15 minutes. Remove from heat
to cool.

When mixture is cool, blend in a blender. Remove to a mixing bowl and stir
in nuts. Whip cream until stiff and fold into mixture. Serve with carob chips
on top (although they're almost superfluous at this point).
Serves 6.

Embracing Mother Earth

*Apricots come in many forms: sulfured, unsulfured, imported, local,
organic, conventional. We each live on the spectrum and get to
choose how far along it we're willing to spend our money and our efforts.
Regardless, apricots are worth it; they're one of the fruits highest in iron,
a boon for those who want extra energy. Be careful in doubling this recipe.
Too much orange peel can turn it bitter, but the flavor is wonderful anyway.
Enjoy!*

Sweet Shepherd's Pie

View of the Whole

Shepherds live well when they eat this! It takes full advantage of seasonal variations in vegetables, and as the holidays approach it reminds of other shepherds in our cultural past.

1 lb. broccoli
4 carrots, diced
1 green pepper, diced
2 Tbsp. unrefined vegetable oil
½ tsp. basil
1 tsp. Bragg's Liquid Aminos
¾ cup chopped fresh tomatoes
1 bunch spinach (or other greens)
4 medium sweet potatoes, cooked & mashed
½ cup milk
1 Tbsp. butter
paprika

Cut broccoli into flowerets. Sauté broccoli, carrots and pepper in oil 5 minutes. Add basil, liquid aminos and tomatoes. Cook 10 minutes longer. Wash spinach well, chop and stir into mixture. Then pour off excess liquid and put vegetables into a 9" x 13" baking dish. Meanwhile, prepare mashed sweet potatoes with milk and 1 Tbsp. butter. Spread over vegetables and bake at 350° for 15 minutes until heated through. Shake paprika on top before serving.
Serves 4-6.

Embracing Mother Earth

Yams and sweet potatoes are not the same. Sweet potatoes are used worldwide as an important carbohydrate; their food value is significantly higher than that of yams. You may still choose yams, especially if this is served with other high-value foods, but be aware of the difference. In either case, the sweetness of the topping is an added treat to this old favorite recipe. When fresh tomatoes are too pricey, tomato paste and some vegetable stock or water are a good alternative. Although the vegetables listed work particularly well together, you can use other vegetables in season or available to you.
Enjoy!

Shortbread Supreme

View of the Whole

*Holidays are often a time of over eating, over sweeting
ourselves, while the origins of holiday sweets have been lost. As we give
sweets to one another, let's use them as reminders to keep our thoughts
and words sweet. This recipe, while far from calorie-less, does keep the
sweetness to a minimum while providing a tasty offering to those we serve.*

1 cup butter, at room temperature
½ cup brown sugar (or part honey)
1⅔ cups unbleached white flour
⅓ cup rice flour
grated peel of one orange (optional)
½ tsp. lemon extract (optional)

Cream together butter and sugar until smooth. Add other ingredients and
mix until dough is smooth, but do not overwork it. Pat into a pie pan or
other container about that size, pressing it to form a smooth, solid shape.
Bake at 325° for 45 minutes, or until shortbread is slightly browned and
still somewhat springy to the touch. Cool 15 minutes before moving to
a serving plate. Cut into pie-shaped wedges.
Serves 8.

Options:

You may add sliced almonds (not too many or shortbread will not hold together),
and other flavorings, such as coconut. Date sugar or brown rice syrup powder may
replace the brown sugar. Part whole wheat pastry flour may be used, but the texture
will be different; the same is true if all unbleached and no rice flour is used. Melting
the butter first makes the creaming easier, but also affects the texture.

Embracing Mother Earth

*The simplicity of this recipe allows maximum opportunity for creativity.
It reminds us as well of the simplicity of all food and our nourishment.
When we look at too many ingredients at once or a lot of Mother Earth at once,
we lose that sense of simplicity that is her most valuable teaching.
So it's important to be aware of simplicity in our creative variations
as we cook—this or anything else. However you vary the theme,
the result can still be supreme. . .
enjoyment.*

Lemon-Yellow Pea Soup

View of the Whole

*Soup's on! Great words to say and to hear during cold weather.
Green split pea soup is well known but its cousin, using yellow peas, is less so.
This has the added pleasure and freshness of lemon, to remind us to keep our own
thoughts and words as fresh as the new-fallen snow.*

**2 cups yellow split peas
8 cups vegetable stock or water
bay leaf
2 Tbsp. butter
1 Tbsp. unrefined vegetable oil
1 carrot, diced
1 stalk celery, diced
1 tsp. Bragg's Liquid Aminos
1 Tbsp. cumin seeds, ground
black pepper
grated peel and juice of 2 lemons
paprika
fresh parsley**

Simmer peas and bay leaf in stock until soft, about 45 minutes. Meanwhile, melt butter with oil and sauté carrot and celery. Add liquid aminos, spices and lemon. Top with paprika and parsley.
Serves 6-8.

Embracing Mother Earth

*Our Earth Mother provides for us in all seasons. Drying beans and peas
is a good way to preserve them; buying them in bulk saves packaging
and allows us to buy just what we need. Other mild vegetables could be included,
but it's important to keep this soup gentle so its subtle flavors mingle and come
through to your eaters' taste buds.
Enjoy!*

Homemade Banana Frozen Yogurt

View of the Whole

*This creation serves as a good alternative to commercial frozen yogurt.
As we constantly seek alternatives to being "out there" in the world
and enjoying our inner life more, we do the same with our foods.
This is a good way to remember both.*

1 banana
½ unpeeled apple
1½ Tbsp. unsulfured molasses
juice from ½ lemon
1 tsp. vanilla
1 cup yogurt

Cut banana and apple in pieces and blend in blender with other ingredients until smooth. Pour into large pan and cover. Freeze until firm, about 3 hours. Remove from pan and blend again at low speed until slightly softened. *Serves 4.*

Embracing Mother Earth

*This light dessert works well with
a heavy meal—easy to fix, easy to digest.
Enjoy!*

Potato Pizza

View of the Whole

*Our Western infatuation with pizza makes a transformation
in this tasty variation. As we learn to transform
our familiar thoughts into new directions,
we can also create tastier inner food.*

3 cups cubed potatoes
1 large, ripe tomato, chopped finely
½ cup tomato paste
1 Tbsp. unrefined vegetable oil
2 tsp. oregano
1 cup ricotta cheese
½ cup grated mozzarella cheese

Steam unpeeled potatoes 20 minutes or until soft. Mash, adding whole wheat flour if needed so they are stiff. Spread on a buttered cookie sheet. Bake in a 400° oven for 15 minutes while preparing sauce.

Combine chopped tomato, tomato paste, oil and oregano. Add a few Tbsp. of potato cooking liquid or tomato purée if needed to make a spreadable consistency. Black olives, chopped Jerusalem artichokes (or sunchoke), green pepper, celery and other niceties may also be added.

Spread ricotta cheese evenly over potato crust. Top with sauce and sprinkle with mozzarella. Return to the oven for 15 more minutes.
Serves 4-6.

Embracing Mother Earth

*Few ingredients feel more "Earthy" than potatoes. In winter months our bodies
seem to crave them more for the sustenance to handle the weather.
This dish meets those needs, as well as our need to honor our bodies with more
healthful food. Mother yourself and
enjoy it!*

Spicy Banana Bake

View of the Whole

*Smelling the aromas of fruit and spices creates anticipation
of the coming meal. Applying that principle, we can enjoy
the process of creating new thoughts by using internal
recipes to create aromas that engage our minds.*

**4 bananas
2 Tbsp. lemon juice
½ cup fruit jam, like orange marmalade
1 tsp. allspice
¼ cup fruit juice or water
¼ cup raisins
¼ cup dried papaya, diced
2 Tbsp. chopped nuts**

Peel bananas; slice in half lengthwise and roll in lemon juice so they won't turn dark. Lay flat on shallow baking pan. Combine other ingredients except nuts and simmer 5 minutes. Pour over bananas. Broil until bananas are hot, about 5 minutes. Watch carefully or the raisins will burn. Spoon sauce over bananas once or twice during broiling. Top with nuts before serving. *Serves 4 (or 8 as a side dish).*

Embracing Mother Earth

*Bananas, high in potassium, are a healthful as well as elegant
part of a meal when prepared this way. It's so easy you can take extra time
in the garden or in quiet thought, instead of working hard to prepare a meal.
Enjoy!*

Savory Stew

View of the Whole

Food that stews blends flavors so they meld into a delicacy.
When we "stew" over something, we may simmer about it
for a long time. Maybe we can learn something from our food.

1 cup dry garbanzo beans	½ green pepper, chopped
1 tsp. cumin seeds	2 Tbsp. unrefined vegetable oil
1 Tbsp. nutritional yeast	1½ cups tomatoes, chopped
vegetable stock or water	1 cup mushrooms, sliced
1 medium red potato, cubed	1 tsp. basil
1 turnip, cubed	1 Tbsp. Bragg's Liquid Aminos
2 tsp. curry powder	¼ tsp. black pepper
1 tsp. paprika	
1 stalk celery, chopped	

Soak garbanzos overnight; drain and cover with vegetable stock or fresh water. Add cumin seeds and cook 2½ hours. Add yeast, potato and turnip; season with curry and paprika, and simmer 45 minutes.

Meanwhile, sauté celery and green pepper in oil for 5 minutes. Add tomatoes, mushrooms and other herbs, and simmer 5 more minutes. Set aside until beans are done; then add to bean mixture, and heat just until stew is hot.
Serves 4-6.

Embracing Mother Earth

A hearty winter supper that whets appetites as it simmers
on the stove. Vary ingredients to suit what's available and in season.
Jerusalem artichokes are a crunchy addition to replace green pepper
if you haven't frozen any and their price is out of sight at the store. Canned
tomatoes can be used; add a fresh one just to "freshen" the pot.
Enjoy!

Holiday Carrot Cake

View of the Whole

*Holidays call for special treats, and it's important to
treat ourselves well at the same time with good nutrition, good taste and
easy preparation. Creating the atmosphere of celebration within our own
thoughts goes a long way toward inviting others to share our space.*

¼ cup honey
1 cup grated raw carrot
1 cup raisins (or part dates)
1 tsp. cinnamon
1 tsp. nutmeg
½ tsp. cloves
½ cup butter
1 cup fruit juice
2 cups whole wheat pastry flour
2 tsp. baking soda
¾ cup chopped nuts and sunflower seeds
2 Tbsp. poppy seeds (optional)

Combine honey, carrot, raisins, spices, butter and juice. Bring to a boil and
boil 5 minutes, stirring. Cool until lukewarm, about 45 minutes (30 minutes
set outside in the snow). Mix dry ingredients; add cooled mixture and stir
thoroughly. Pour into a well-buttered 9" x 13" baking pan. Bake at 350°
for 40 minutes or until it tests done. Cool and frost with Cream Cheese
Frosting (pg. 123) or serve with plain yogurt.
Serves 8-12.

Embracing Mother Earth

*Putting together each ingredient from its natural state enhances the
joy of any recipe. This is no exception and the taste can never compare to any
prepackaged alternative. Enjoy the simplicity of cooking from the basics and regain
connection with the ingredients that go into the food you eat and serve.
Enjoy!*

Nancy's Kale Soup

View of the Whole

*When we allow different ingredients of life to blend together, we can be
surprised at the beneficial results. If we try to plan the blend, it rarely works
as well as accepting what happens. In the kitchen this soup is a good example.*

2 Tbsp. unrefined vegetable oil
½ tsp. mustard seeds
½ tsp. cumin seeds
7 cups vegetable stock or water
2 cups carrots, sliced in rounds
2 cups sweet potato, cubed
1 cup lentils
2-4 cups kale, sliced in strips

Heat oil in a large pan and roast seeds until they pop. Add 4 cups of stock
with carrots and sweet potatoes. Bring to a boil and simmer 30 minutes.
Meanwhile, cook lentils in 3 cups of stock for 1 hour (until mushy). Mix lentils
and vegetables and add kale. Cook 5-10 minutes. Add liquid aminos to taste
if you wish.
Serves 6-8.

Embracing Mother Earth

*Experiment with the proportions of vegetables to suit your
own taste, available ingredients and creativity. Kale is a highly nutritious
vegetable that deserves more use. It's an easy vegetable to grow—flourishing
in many climates all winter, making it an especially beneficial boost toward feeding
ourselves from our gardens year-round.*
Enjoy!

Jenny's Poppyseed Prune Bread

View of the Whole

Another cook lost to posterity—except in name—but thanks Jenny, wherever you are. Sometimes just the name of a recipe is enough to start salivation. This one did so for me, and perhaps knowing that will encourage you to experiment with it. So much in life happens this way. From the joyful experience of another, we find that we too learn something new.

3 cups vegetable stock or fruit juice
¼ cup unrefined vegetable oil
¼ cup honey
2 Tbsp. molasses
2 tsp. sea salt
3 cups rolled oats
1 cup sunflower seeds
½ cup poppy seeds
1 cup prunes, pitted and diced
½ tsp. cinnamon
¼ tsp. nutmeg
8-9 cups whole wheat flour

Heat liquid; stir in oil, honey and molasses. Add salt and oats; let it sit while you toast the seeds in a dry skillet and dice the prunes. Add spices and then gradually add flour. Knead the resulting huge glob of dough (in two batches if one is too heavy) at least 300 times, or until it stays together and can be shaped into a round. Bake at 300° for 1½ hours or until firm-crusted and deep brown in color. This bread keeps well and gets better with age. *Serves 8-10.*

Embracing Mother Earth

Toasting seeds or nuts before using them adds a stronger flavor. It's easy to do and makes a special treat when topping a main dish or dessert. Simply put them in a dry skillet and stir constantly until they smell good. Remove from heat immediately as they burn quickly once they toast.
Enjoy!

Decadent Cabbage

View of the Whole

*Winter months bring vegetables like cabbage to the fore. They grow
in cold weather, warm the body and the spirit, and steam up the kitchen
in the process. Paying conscious attention to the tightly circled leaves
around the firm core is a way to focus our attention on our own core,
surrounded by the leaves of all the beings in our lives.*

12 cups chopped cabbage (about 2 lbs.)
3 Tbsp. unrefined vegetable oil
4 Tbsp. whole wheat flour
2 tsp. nutritional yeast
2 cups milk
1 tsp. dill weed
Bragg's Liquid Aminos to taste
1½ cups cottage cheese
2 cups whole-grain bread crumbs

Steam cabbage in a large pan until tender but still crisp. Heat oil in a skillet;
stir in flour and yeast. Add milk slowly; then stir until thick. Add dill and liquid
aminos.

In a large oiled casserole layer cabbage, cottage cheese, bread crumbs and
sauce, ending with sauce and a topping of crumbs. Bake at 350° for 30-
40 minutes.
Serves 6 as a main dish.

Embracing Mother Earth

*Herbs like dill add a fragrance to both winter and summer. Plan now to
grow some in your own garden. Their beautiful leafy fronds and rounded
seed heads are a joy to watch. When the seeds ripen, simply cut the whole
stem and put it in a large paper bag. When dry, gently pull off the greenery
and seal into one container and the ripe seeds in another. Then you have your
own fragrance to use in dishes like this next winter.*
Enjoy!

Healthful Carrot Cake

View of the Whole

*In the midst of holiday eating, this raw "cake" gives our stomachs a break
and adds a crunchy pleasure that slows down eating. It's a good time to
remember that food is here to serve us, not the other way around. As we prepare
each ingredient, we add our love to the process. The closer we can come to
natural fruits and vegetables, the closer we realize the beauty of life's simplicity.*

**3 cups carrots, garated
1 cup soaked, chopped dry fruit
1 cup nuts, chopped
½ cup honey
1 tsp. cinnamon
¼ tsp. nutmeg
wheat germ (optional)**

Mix ingredients together, adding wheat germ if necessary so mixture is not
too moist. Press into a rounded bowl and turn out onto a plate. Chill well to
set shape. For a festive air, you can frost this with yogurt sprinkled with nuts.
Serves 8.

Embracing Mother Earth

*Carrots are a basic ingredient to winter cooking.
Not only do they overwinter in the garden, they can be obtained easily since
they survive cold storage well. When buying even organic carrots, watch the
tops. If they are starting to sprout, it means they've been kept in cold storage
quite awhile; choose again. Let the carrots talk to you; feel the ones that have
an aliveness to them. They're the ones who want to come home with you
and share this meal.
Enjoy!*

Polenta Bake

View of the Whole

*Many people think of polenta as a Mexican dish, but it's actually the
Italian way of using coarse-ground cornmeal. We often take items like this for
granted and rarely check their origins. It makes one wonder how many other things
in life we take for granted and do not check out to inform ourselves. Savoring this
dish, savor also the thought of being more conscious of the textures and tastes of
foods, both familiar and unfamiliar.*

**1 Tbsp. butter
4 cups vegetable stock or water
1½ cups coarse cornmeal (polenta)
½ cup Monterey jack cheese
1 tsp. thyme**

Melt butter in boiling stock. Stir in cornmeal. Cook at low heat for 25
minutes, stirring constantly. It will become very thick. Turn polenta into
a greased pan, smooth the top and set it aside to cool. Top with slices
of cheese and sprinkle with thyme. Bake at 350° for 25 minutes or until
heated through and cheese melts. Serve with hot Savory Vegetable
Sauce, (pg. 84).
Serves 4-6.

Options:

You can also slice the polenta and fry it in butter, or layer it in a casserole with a
mushroom sauce and cheese. It has many possibilities for something so easy and
makes a satisfying, simple main course any time of year.

Embracing Mother Earth

*Handling the ingredients while cooking provides a direct
connection with the Earth. We can learn nature's lessons
with each step we take in the kitchen.
Enjoy!*

Apple Delight

View of the Whole

*Easy apple recipes abound but it's fun to find
a new one that's even easier and tastier than the usual "crisps."
We forget the simple things in life, thinking we have to create something
complicated to "succeed." Instead, delight in the apples; enjoy the time to
do other things and share this along with the rest
and relaxation that result from its easy preparation.*

4 cups unpeeled apples, chopped
¼ cup honey (or to taste)
½ cup apple juice
1 tsp. vanilla
1 tsp. cinnamon
¼ tsp. cloves
¼ tsp. nutmeg
¼ lb. tofu
½ cup milk
½ cup whole wheat flour

Place chopped apples in a 9" x 9" baking dish. Top with honey. Place other ingredients, except flour, in a blender and mix until smooth. Pour over apples. Add flour and mix well. Bake at 375° until set, approximately 60 minutes.
Serves 6-8. (This recipe doubles easily; bake in a 9" x 13" pan.)

Options:

You can also add ½ cup raisins for additional iron. Nuts are another good addition, though not needed if the main dish contains nuts.

Embracing Mother Earth

*Add the cores of organic apples to your soup-stock pot. They add a
good flavor and give your apples another way to help your diet. Besides,
they compost more quickly after cooking.
Enjoy!*

Morning or Night Cabbage and Tofu

View of the Whole

*Our culture is conditioned to sweets for breakfast, unlike
other parts of the world. To wean yourself from that habit, try this for
breakfast sometime. It's consciously changing our habits that allows us to
view them as a choice, which in turn strengthens our own self-awareness and
self-respect. We then begin to act from a place of power, rather than feeling
caught in habits that seem unchangeable.*

**1 lb. tofu
1 Tbsp. unrefined vegetable oil
1 Tbsp. sesame oil
1 tsp. turmeric
1 Tbsp. fresh ginger, grated
small head of cabbage, shredded
1 Tbsp. Bragg's Liquid Aminos
sesame seeds**

Cut tofu into small cubes. Sauté in oils, turmeric and ginger until brown, about 10 minutes. Remove from the skillet, add a bit more oil, and cook cabbage over medium heat until tender, about 10 minutes. Add liquid aminos and tofu mixture, then toss. Serve hot, over steamed brown rice; top with sesame seeds.

Options:
Another delightful addition is a handful of sprouted garbanzo beans, to cook with the cabbage. You can experiment with other herbs and spices as well.

Embracing Mother Earth

*This delicious entrée comes together quickly and
satisfies winter appetites with its heartiness. No need to throw away any of
the outer leaves of cabbage. They've already been trimmed down before you buy
them, and if you grow them, you know how good they are from the outermost to
the innermost bite. What you don't use directly can go into the soup-stock
savings for another use.*
Enjoy!

Happy Apple Bread

View of the Whole

Apples always seem like happy fruit to me. When we experience fruit that way, we increase our own inner well-being and share that energy with all who share the food with us.

2 cups whole wheat pastry flour
1 Tbsp. baking powder
2 tsp. cinnamon
¼ cup yogurt
½ cup milk
¼ cup unrefined vegetable oil
⅓ cup honey
1 cup finely chopped apple
½ cup raisins (optional)

Preheat oven to 400°. Stir the dry ingredients together. Combine wet ingredients and add the dry ingredients and mix. Gently fold in apples and raisins. Pour into buttered 9" x 9" baking dish and bake 30-35 minutes, or until cake tester in the center comes out clean.

Options:
Moist and delicious, this bread is a great start to a day or ending to a dinner. You can also make muffins from this recipe; bake them 20-25 minutes.
Serves 9.

Embracing Mother Earth

Apples are delicious in any form, provide beauty in every season, and on the practical level add digestive enzymes to our meals. The smell of apple bread baking is sure to increase the appetites of those who share it, another good reason for making it.
Enjoy!

Barley and Lentil Stew

View of the Whole

Combining grains, like combining thoughts, often leads to a more wholesome result. But first we must learn what combines well and what becomes more productive as a result. With food we can taste or sniff as we go; with thoughts the process is more subtle.

½ cup dried lentils
½ cup celery, chopped
¼ cup butter (or half unrefined vegetable oil)
2½ cups tomatoes, chopped
⅓ cup whole barley
1 Tbsp. Bragg's Liquid Aminos
¼ tsp. black pepper
2 tsp. rosemary, crushed
2 cups vegetable stock or water
¼ cup fresh parsley, chopped
½ cup carrots, shredded

Soak lentils in water several hours to shorten cooking time, if desired; drain. Meanwhile, in a large pan sauté celery in butter (and oil, if used) for 5 minutes. Add remaining ingredients except carrots, bring to a boil, cover and simmer for 30 minutes, stirring occasionally. Add carrots and cook 5 minutes longer.
Serves 4.

Options:
Crunchy French bread goes well with this stew. Fresh tomatoes are best, in season, but canned purée works well also, making this a good dish for any season. Adding the carrots at the end gives a freshness to the stew, and they cook quickly since they've been shredded. Fresh mushrooms would be another good last-minute addition.

Embracing Mother Earth

A simple pleasure for a cool evening, but keep the combinations simple so you can savor the flavors as they mingle.
Enjoy!

Apple Crisp

View of the Whole

It's a constant source of amazement how many variations there are to basic recipes like this. In the same way we can amaze ourselves with the number of variations on a single thought, when we pause long enough to play with it and turn it to see its many aspects. Time spent slicing apples is a good opportunity to think about a thought this way.

5-6 cups unpeeled sliced apples
1½ cups nuts, chopped
¼ cup honey, or to taste
1 cup apple juice or water
1 cup whole wheat flour
⅓ cup butter
2 tsp. cinnamon
1 Tbsp. unsulfured molasses
yogurt

Place apple slices in a 9" x 13" buttered baking pan. Sprinkle with nuts and drizzle on honey to taste. Pour juice over all. In a bowl, mix flour and butter until it is like cornmeal. Add cinnamon and molasses and sprinkle over apple mixture. Cover and bake 30 minutes at 400°. Uncover and bake 10 minutes longer or until top browns slightly. Serve with yogurt.
Serves 6.

Embracing Mother Earth

This is a great way to use windfall apples or ones that have been stored for some time. The good parts of any apples that are left make a good base for this dessert and save both energy and other resources.
Enjoy!

Brenda's Baked Tofu

View of the Whole

*Long time friends (some just met recently) are a good source of great recipes.
We in turn are good sources of our own internal recipes for friends who seek
our "food." Ponder this while you create this yummy entrée,
remembering as you put it in the oven that you are also firing
your own imagination to create newness in your life.*

2 lb. firm tofu
½ cup Bragg's Liquid Aminos
¼ cup rice vinegar
2 Tbsp. olive oil
1 Tbsp. tahini
½ tsp. Dijon mustard
1 Tbsp. grated fresh ginger
water (optional)
2 Tbsp. sesame seeds
1 Tbsp. nutritional yeast

Drain and cut tofu into ½" thick slices. Lay slices on a towel and press
something flat down on top of the slices, to remove excess liquid. Mix other
ingredients (except seeds and yeast) in a deep baking dish; marinate tofu
in this mixture as long as possible, preferably all day. Drain and place
slices on a buttered cookie sheet. Sprinkle with seeds and yeast. Bake at
375° for 30-45 minutes.
Serves 6, with brown rice and a green vegetable.

Embracing Mother Earth

*When the sun's out and the Earth is warming, we are called outdoors and spend
even less time in the kitchen. This dish is a good choice then, for you can start it
easily, let it sit while you're enjoying the sunshine, and then easily bake it with
little effort at dinnertime, while preparing the other parts of the meal.
Enjoy!*

Carrot Surprise Soup

View of the Whole

*It's good to surprise ourselves with foods. Sometimes we know all the
ingredients, but hadn't thought of putting them together. That's the same
process as creating new ideas—the components may all have been there before,
but we see a new way to combine them and create something new.*

½ cup unsulfured dried apricots
1 cup apple juice
8 carrots, sliced thinly
2 cups vegetable stock or water
1 tsp. Bragg's Liquid Aminos
1 Tbsp. parsley, chopped
1 tsp. dill weed
1 Tbsp. tahini (sesame butter)
1 Tbsp. yogurt
½-1 cup cooked soybeans or garbanzos

Simmer apricots in apple juice 5 minutes. Let them stand in juice until soup
is ready. Meanwhile, combine carrots, stock, liquid aminos, parsley and dill
in a large pan and simmer 15 minutes. Place apricot mixture and half the
carrot mixture in a blender with tahini and yogurt. Blend until smooth.
Combine with remaining carrots and beans.
Serve hot, to 4.

Options:
For a soup that's less sweet, you can substitute vegetable stock for the apple juice.

Embracing Mother Earth

*If you like sprouts, use them in this soup. But plan a couple days ahead,
so you can sprout the beans yourself. Otherwise, substitute canned beans and add
them before serving. With the sweetness of the apple juice and apricots this soup
doubles as dessert and also makes a fine main lunch dish, as well as a part
of dinner. The balance of flavors is delicate, so keep it simple and
enjoy!*

Aloo Gobhi Variation

View of the Whole

Staples get overly familiar in the diet. Near winter's end is a good time to experiment with different spices to give them a new taste. In the same way our thought patterns can get lazy. It's important to make an opportunity periodically (especially after "gloomy" times) to spice them up with new ideas, new experiences.

1 Tbsp. unrefined vegetable oil
1 tsp. mustard seeds
1 Tbsp. cumin seeds
1 tsp. ground ginger
1 tsp. chili powder
1 tsp. turmeric
1 medium cauliflower, divided into small flowerets
4 potatoes
1 Tbsp. Bragg's Liquid Aminos
¼ cup vegetable stock or water
¼ cup yogurt, or to taste

Heat oil in a large heavy pan. Add seeds, stirring until they begin to pop. Add other spices, then cauliflower, potatoes, liquid aminos and stock. Stir to mix evenly. Cover and simmer about 15 minutes, until done but still crisp. Stir in yogurt, and serve hot or at room temperature.
Serves 4 as a main course with brown rice. It can also be used as a side dish.

Embracing Mother Earth

Popping seeds before using them gives them a toasted flavor, an easy way to vary the dishes you prepare. New flavors bring new opportunities to pay attention to our cooking process.
Enjoy!

Apple Pastry

View of the Whole

*As we find our rightful place in the scheme of things,
we shift our tastes accordingly. During this transition called
life, we try out these shifts and feel them in new ways. Cooking
ingredients such as butter are no exception.*

For dough:

**2 cups whole wheat pastry flour
1 tsp. baking powder
¼ tsp. sea salt
¼ cup butter at room temperature
1 tsp. vanilla**

Stir together dry ingredients. Add butter and vanilla; blend with a fork, then fingers, until it forms a dough. Flatten into a round and wrap in waxed paper. Refrigerate at least 15 minutes. Remove from refrigerator and work until it softens a little. Roll out on waxed paper into approximately 8" x 14".

For filling:

**3 cups apples, thinly sliced
2 tsp. cinnamon
juice and grated peel of one lemon
⅓ cup raisins
1-2 Tbsp. honey (or to taste)
yogurt (optional topping)**

Mix all filling ingredients. Place along one long edge of dough. Using waxed paper to help, roll dough and seal ends. Slide onto baking pan. Bake at 325° until light brown, about 45 minutes. Offer yogurt as a topping.
Serves 4-6.

Embracing Mother Earth

*Apples are a wonderful standby during the winter when we miss
the varieties of fresh fruit. Their crispness is a welcome snack and baking them
with cinnamon into a luscious pastry warms the nostrils and the kitchen.
Enjoy!*

Adzuki Beans and Pasta

View of the Whole

Beans and wheat combine to improve the protein potency of a meal. Broccoli is one of the most nutritious vegetables, so its inclusion in this recipe makes it a super-energizing meal. Combining our thoughts into nutritious forms makes them super-energizing as well, and we can always create more of them while cooking dinner.

½ lb. whole wheat spaghetti
2 Tbsp. unrefined vegetable oil
2 tsp. garam masala* or other herb mixture
2 cups broccoli flowerets
2 large tomatoes, chopped
2 cups cooked adzuki beans
1 Tbsp. freshly grated ginger root
2 Tbsp. dark miso
2 Tbsp. cornstarch
1 cup warm vegetable stock or water
2 tsp. sesame oil

Cook pasta, drain and set aside. Meanwhile, heat and season oil with garam masala or other herb. Sauté broccoli in the oil, covered, 2-3 minutes. Add tomatoes, beans and ginger. Simmer 10 minutes.

In a small bowl, stir miso, cornstarch and stock until smooth. Pour into skillet with sesame oil; simmer gently to thicken, about 10 minutes. Add sauce mixture to pasta; combine thoroughly.
Serves 4.

* Garam Masala is a combination of spices commonly used in East Indian recipes. Like curry, it's not a specific combination but takes various forms.

Embracing Mother Earth

Unusual pasta combinations remind us that we can invent meals any time we choose. Mother Earth teaches us that in every move— recombining, rejoining colors and tastes in gay abandon as the seasons change. Springtime will soon burst with energy and we embrace it in our cooking.
Enjoy!

Molasses Cake

View of the Whole

*As spring approaches, it's spring tonic time! Earlier generations knew to
add iron-rich foods in the early spring, as the bright greens become available.
An alternative was to add more molasses (and raisins) to baked goods.
Funny how that feeling stays with us, and this molasses recipe looks irresistible
this time of year. As we learn to tune into our spiritual strength in similar ways,
we begin to make deeper choices to use our energy more meaningfully.
Think about it while stirring this easy cake.*

**2½ cups whole wheat flour
1½ tsp. baking soda
½ cup unrefined vegetable oil
½ cup unsulfured molasses
¼ cup blackstrap molasses
½ cup hot water
yogurt (optional topping)**

Combine flour and baking soda in large bowl. Stir in oil and molasses. Take
out and save one cup of this mixture. In a small bowl combine the blackstrap
and hot water. Add to the flour mixture and stir thoroughly. Pour the batter
into a lightly buttered 9" x 9" pan. Sprinkle reserved cup of flour mixture on
top. Bake at 375° for 25-30 minutes, or until it tests done.
Serves 6-8.

Options:

This is not a sweet cake, and serves well as a different breakfast treat as well as for
after dinner. Either time, it's great with yogurt on top. If you run short of either kind
of molasses, you can substitute a little honey.

Embracing Mother Earth

*Molasses is basically unrefined sugar, straight from the cane before the life is
processed out of it. Blackstrap is the nearest to cane; unsulfured (medium is
better than light) at least retains some minerals. In any case, enjoy your tonic
that gives you extra energy to get ready for spring!
Enjoy!*

Lavish Limas

View of the Whole

How often we take for granted basic foods like dried beans.
Yet they too can become delightful treats when we search out combinations of
ingredients that enhance their natural qualities. We are each that "dried
bean" and have natural qualities when we use ourselves effectively in
combinations that enhance who we really are.

1 cup dried limas* or small white beans
5 cups vegetable stock or water
¾ cup brown rice, uncooked
1¼ cups prunes, halved
4 large carrots, sliced in thin rounds
2 tsp. cinnamon
1 Tbsp. Bragg's Liquid Aminos
2 Tbsp. honey
1 Tbsp. lemon juice

Cover beans with cold water and soak overnight. Drain and add vegetable stock. Cook *uncovered* for 30 minutes. Add rice, prunes, carrots and cinnamon and cook for 60 minutes longer. Add liquid aminos and honey; cook another 30 minutes or until stew is thick and ingredients tender. Stir in lemon juice just before serving. As a meal in itself, with a green salad if you wish, it doesn't even need a dessert.
Serves 4-6.

*Lima beans, unlike other beans, contain enough potentially toxic cyanide compounds that they require special cooking attention. Boil in an uncovered pot and the cyanide gas will escape in the steam. Prepare all lima beans— fresh, dried, or sprouted—this way.

Embracing Mother Earth

Another multi-cultural delight, this stew is similar
to those found on tables in eastern Europe. Besides the high protein value of
the beans, especially in combination with rice, it includes high iron value in
the prunes. Another way to enjoy prunes is to layer them in a quart glass jar
with thin slices of fresh lemon. Fill the jar with boiling water; cover and
let it sit for 24 hours.
Enjoy!

Creamy Fresh Salad Dressing

View of the Whole

*The fresh taste of this dressing goes a long way to freshen up a cooked
meal and to remind us that the thoughts that speak from our heart
go a long way toward bringing a freshness to our communications as well.*

**2 Tbsp. fresh lemon juice
1 tsp. Bragg's Liquid Aminos
½ cup yogurt
¼ cup unrefined vegetable oil
 (half olive oil if you prefer)
black pepper to taste
1 tsp. oregano
1 tsp. honey (optional)**

Shake together in a jar. May be stored in the refrigerator for a week.
Makes 1 cup, enough for 4-6 servings.

Embracing Mother Earth

*There is no substitute for using fresh ingredients. As we learn to
incorporate more fresh, raw foods into our diet, we feel better on many
levels. The foods then begin to work on subtle levels to create more
peace and joy in our lives beyond the dining table.*
Enjoy!

Spring

Just two feet of garden
a place to plant a few carrots
in ceremony
the ritual of spring
the renewal of connections
with the Earth
the seeds
sprinkled gently
on the still-wet soil
as the earthworms turn
wriggling to hide again
get back to work
the seeds
patted firmly
and covered with old straw
to do their work
the seeds
remembered
as thoughts of growth
renewal
starting fresh
with the season's turn
wriggling to be born
and get to work
in the space of this moment
tilling the soil
of my mind

—h.k.

Golden Bean Soup

View of the Whole

*A great way to make the transition between seasons is with a soup,
hearty but not heavy. The golden color of this one is an added attraction.
In the spring sunshine the goldenness of our glow is also an added attraction,
helping us bloom with increased heartiness.*

1½ cups dried small white beans
10 cups vegetable stock or water
2 cups cubed yams, unpeeled
2 Tbsp. basil
¼ cup Bragg's Liquid Aminos
¼ cup fresh parsley, chopped
dash of cayenne pepper
1 stalk of celery, chopped
½ cup carrots, sliced
1 cup broccoli, chopped

Soak beans in water overnight; drain and add the vegetable stock. Mix in
other ingredients, except broccoli. Bring to a boil and simmer uncovered
until beans are tender, about 2½ hours. Add broccoli only for the last half-
hour.
Makes 12 cups, which serves 6-8 as a main course.

Options:
This soup is terrific, especially when served over Ceremonial Cornbread (pg. 31).

Embracing Mother Earth

*Growing your own parsley is an easy way to add a personal,
fresh, flavorful touch to dishes any time of year. Growing
a pot of parsley or other herb on the windowsill is one
way to say who you are, how you care for yourself
and the others you feed.*
Enjoy!

Easiest Dessert Ever

View of the Whole

*When it's a matter of time and of enjoying company (your own or others'),
try this idea. Time isn't what matters anyway; it's enjoying company and the food
we share together, be it in our thoughts of others or in their presence.*

Peel a banana. Freeze on a cookie sheet until hard. At serving time, slice
the banana into a dessert dish. Top with shredded coconut, raisins, nuts,
yogurt, whatever you like.

Serves 1+, depending on how hungry you are.

For special occasions, top with something like this easy sauce:

Carob for Dessert

**1 cup water
2 Tbsp. honey
2 tsp. vanilla
2 Tbsp. cornstarch
1 Tbsp. unrefined vegetable oil
1 tsp. decaffeinated coffee powder** (optional)
2 Tbsp. roasted carob powder

Mix all ingredients and bring to a boil, stirring constantly. Remove from heat
when thickened.
Makes 1¼ cups, enough for 6 servings of Easiest Dessert Ever.

Embracing Mother Earth

*When bananas ripen faster than they are eaten, they can be quickly peeled
and frozen to have on hand for this delightful dessert. They can also be blended
with some yogurt and apple juice for a refreshing drink. It's an old wives' tale
that you can't refrigerate bananas. When they're as ripe as you like,
refrigerate them. The skin will turn dark but the fruit will stay firm.
They're sweetest when ripe and best used then anyway.
Enjoy!*

Greek Spinach Stew

View of the Whole

*As the world begins to green toward spring, our thoughts turn to
fresh greens; yet winter weather and vegetables persist, and the body wants
heavier sustenance like rice. This easy recipe combines both, a good
transition dish for late winter/early spring. In the same way, we find ways to
combine our inner, still hibernating patterns with those of opening up to the
warming air. We can be outdoors more, breathe more deeply, start to clean
house—inner and outer—before spring calls us outdoors more. It's time to
reflect on the opening just beginning to happen for each of us.*

2 bunches fresh spinach
¼ cup unrefined vegetable oil
½ tsp. dry mustard
2 tsp. Dijon mustard
4 tomatoes or ½ cup tomato purée
black pepper to taste
¼ cup dill weed or 2 Tbsp. dill seeds
1 Tbsp. Bragg's Liquid Aminos
2 cups vegetable stock or water
1 cup brown rice

Wash and cut spinach finely, stems and all. Sauté in oil with mustards. When
limp, add tomatoes, seasonings and stock; bring to a boil. Add rice, cover
and simmer 1 hour. Stir occasionally and add stock if needed to maintain
consistency of a thick stew.
Serves 4-6.

Embracing Mother Earth

*Depending on the season, other greens, perhaps more plentiful than spinach, may
substitute. This is a meal in itself, either for lunch or for dinner. You may save
half the greens (some leaves, at least) and add them only for the last five minutes
of cooking, so they have that fresh look and taste.
The rest will serve to flavor the rice.
Enjoy!*

Tofu Peanut Butter Cheesecake

View of the Whole

*Healthful cooking that's also
delicious makes easy access to vegetarian fare.
This is one of my favorites. You can easily make a lunch out
of this alone, with plans for a good salad for dinner to complement its high
protein content. When we treat ourselves right, we gain not only self-esteem
but the joy of sharing our good feelings with others we connect with. Radiating
those feelings onward and outward is what it's all about,
in foods as in other parts of our lives.*

**½ cup fruit juice or water
½ cup honey
2 tsp. vanilla
1 16 oz. pkg. tofu
¾ cup peanut butter
carob chips (optional)**

Place ingredients (except chips) in blender in the order listed, to make blending easier. Blend well until smooth. Pour into an unbaked Walnut Crust (pg. 19) lined with carob chips and bake for 25 minutes at 350°. Cool before slicing.

Options:

You can also use ½ cup peanut butter and add ½ cup carob powder instead of carob chips. A sliced banana arranged over the bottom is another good alternative. Without the crust, you can use the filling as a pudding if you prefer.

Embracing Mother Earth

*The use of tofu to replace cream cheese in
delectable desserts like this makes them
worth the small effort of creation. Whatever you create,
enjoy!*

Lentil Griddle Cakes

View of the Whole

This very different recipe brings a new texture and combines unusual tastes for a main course. As the griddle cakes cook, pause a moment to appreciate your own uniqueness and that of others.

1 cup pink lentils
⅓ cup brown rice
7 Tbsp. vegetable stock or water
1 tsp. chili powder
1½ inch piece fresh ginger, grated
½ tsp. sea salt
8 Tbsp. unrefined vegetable oil

Rinse lentils and rice, and put in bowl with enough water to cover by one inch. Soak overnight, then drain. Put in blender with stock, chili, ginger and salt. Purée until mixture is smooth. (Can be prepared a day ahead and refrigerated.)

Heat griddle to medium hot, then oil lightly. Ladle ½ cup of batter onto center of griddle and spread to a 6" round. Make a ½" diameter hole in the center so it will cook more evenly. Cook until dry looking, about 2 minutes. Pour 2 tsp. oil around edge and into center. When the bottom is brown and crisp, 2-3 more minutes, turn and cook on second side.
Serve warm to 4-6, with steamed vegetable or salad.

Options:
Good with hot applesauce or with yogurt. Also good cold if there are any left over.

Embracing Mother Earth

*Lentils need no presoaking before cooking
and cook in a shorter time than beans, making them
an excellent choice for a quickly prepared lunch or dinner.
Enjoy!*

Rice Pudding with Tofu

View of the Whole

*Balance is the key to inner and outer living.
With a lighter meal or one without grains,
this dessert serves as the balance and adds
its own strength of protein as well.*

3 cups cooked brown rice
½ tsp. vanilla
1 cup tofu
¼ tsp. cardamom
3 Tbsp. maple syrup or honey
1 tsp. grated lemon rind
½ cup raisins

Place cooked rice in a large bowl. In a blender combine other ingredients except raisins. Blend until smooth. Pour over rice and add raisins; stir to combine. Chill or heat before serving—good either cold or hot.
Serves 6.

Options:
You can cook the rice in apple juice and omit the maple syrup if you prefer.

Embracing Mother Earth

*The blend of flavors of tofu, lemon and raisins, with cardamom and
maple syrup, is a real treat. A little of this dessert goes a long way.
It might be an easy way to introduce people to tofu,
for its texture is complemented well by the rice.
Enjoy!*

Green Pie

View of the Whole

As we enjoy what's growing as the weather warms, we can focus our thoughts on the warmth of the sun as an example of how we can warm others. Being aware of either process benefits us in many ways.

**2 bunches fresh greens
(Swiss chard, spinach,
kale or combination)
3 cups cottage cheese
1 cup walnuts, chopped**

**2 tsp. garam masala*
or other herb blend
1 Tbsp. Bragg's Liquid Aminos
½ cup grated cheese**

Clean and chop greens; steam lightly. Squeeze out as much liquid as possible and chop again bite-size or smaller. Mix with cottage cheese and chopped walnuts. Sprinkle with garam masala or herbs. Add liquid aminos. Stir. Spoon into a baked Crunchy Pie Shell or over plain mashed potatoes patted into a large baking dish. Top with grated cheese. Bake at 350° for 10 minutes, just to melt the cheese.
Serves 6 but don't count on leftovers.

* See (pg. 108)

Crunchy Pie Shell

**½ cup yellow cornmeal
3 cups whole wheat pastry flour
¾ cup melted butter
¾-1 cup ice water**

Mix dry ingredients. Slowly add butter while mixing with a fork. Add cold water, 1 Tbsp. at a time. When the dough starts to stick together in one mass, form into 3 balls, using your hands. Roll out each between pieces of waxed paper. Place in baking pan or pie pan. Poke gently with a fork in several places. Bake at 350° for 20 minutes or until lightly browned. Makes 3 pie crusts. (For a 9" x 13" pan, use two balls.)

Embracing Mother Earth

When your garden greens get bigger than you prefer to eat as is, try them this way. Enjoy!

Fruit and Dairyless Cream

View of the Whole

With a main course heavy on dairy (if you use dairy at all), it's good to select a dairyless dessert for balance. It's awareness of simple magic like this that brings energy into our meals. It's one way to pay attention to our bodies as we create with our thoughts the environment in which we prefer to live and move and have our being. We feel better, others who share the food with us feel better—even if they don't know the awareness with which we prepared it. Thus the planet Earth herself feels better, for we bring our balance into all that we do.

12 cups fresh fruit, chopped
6 pitted dates, sliced
2 tsp. honey
1 tsp. vanilla
⅔ cup walnuts
½ tsp. cinnamon
⅛ cup fruit juice or water

Chop fresh fruit, sprinkling with fresh lemon juice if needed to keep it from turning dark before serving time. Layer fruit and dates in small dessert dishes.

Nut Cream: Put remaining ingredients into blender and purée until smooth. Spoon over fruit. Serve at room temperature.
Serves 4.

Options:
One good combination is fresh apples and stewed rhubarb. Try your own favorites with this special topping, any time of year.

Embracing Mother Earth

Use whatever fruit is in season as locally as possible, both to provide the best nutrition and to support local growers (especially those who farm organically).
Enjoy!

Simple Stir-fry

View of the Whole

*Stir-fry is like living moment by moment,
enjoying each flavor and
then letting it go.*

½ lb. tofu, cut into cubes
2-4 Tbsp. unrefined vegetable oil
2 tsp. Bragg's Liquid Aminos
1 bunch spinach
2 Tbsp. raisins
pinch of nutmeg
2-4 Tbsp. broken walnuts
4 Tbsp. yogurt

Cook a grain as undergirding, like shortgrain brown rice. In a hot skillet, put 1- 2 Tbsp. oil and sauté the tofu until crispy on the outside, approximately 10 minutes. Add liquid aminos during cooking. Remove tofu and keep warm, uncovered (it will lose its crispness if you cover it).

Wash fresh spinach well and remove stems, saving them for other uses. Add 2 Tbsp. oil to skillet, put in spinach and add raisins (so they will plump during cooking) and nutmeg. Cover and cook over high heat until spinach is limp (3-5 minutes), stirring occasionally. Liquid will boil away in the same time. After cooking, add broken walnuts.To serve, add tofu to cooked spinach. Serve over grain. Top with plain yogurt.
Serves 2.

Options:
Many vegetables can be used instead of spinach, depending on availability. Stir-fry by the same method, choosing herbs that are compatible.

Embracing Mother Earth

*Spinach stems make great soup. Wash them well first. See Cream of Broccoli Soup (pg.114) for general directions. When combining vegetables into a medley, use those that grow together seasonally to harmonize with the way nature grows them. No herbs are needed, though you may add some if you choose.
Enjoy the rainbow!*

Crazy Carob Cake

View of the Whole

*Creating dishes in new ways helps us to see the joy of
using our thoughts in new ways that may seem
"crazy" at first, but have delicious results.*

1½ cups whole wheat pastry flour	6 Tbsp. unrefined vegetable oil
1 tsp. baking soda	½ cup honey
3 Tbsp. toasted carob powder or unsweetened cocoa	1 Tbsp. vinegar
	1 tsp. vanilla
	1 cup cold water

Stir together dry ingredients in an unbuttered 9" x 9" pan. Make three depressions. Distribute oil among the depressions, then the honey, vinegar and vanilla. Pour the cold water over all. Using a slotted spoon or pancake turner, mix ingredients thoroughly. Bake at 350° for 30-35 minutes, or until a toothpick inserted in the center comes out clean.
Serves 8, plain or with Cream Cheese Frosting for special occasions.

Cream Cheese Frosting

8 oz. cream cheese, at room temperature
¼ cup soft butter
¼ cup honey or maple syrup
2½ tsp. vanilla
grated rind of one lemon
2 Tbsp. heavy cream (optional)

Beat together cream cheese and butter until smooth. Add honey, vanilla and lemon rind. If frosting is too thick, add cream to thin. Spread evenly over cake. For a holiday look, add fresh holly leaves (the berries are poisonous!) or fresh flowers.

Embracing Mother Earth

Carob contains no caffeine and is thus a good substitute for chocolate, which contains caffeine. This is a dark, moist cake that goes into the oven quickly once you decide to make it. The description is certainly different from any other cake I've made, but it works.
Enjoy!

Lentils with Love

View of the Whole

*"Love your body," many healers recommend. One way we can do
this is to feed it high-fiber meals that allow its inner toothbrushes to work
most effectively. Positive thoughts are the "high fiber" meals our minds need
to work most effectively, a good thought to ponder while preparing this dish.*

1½ cups dried lentils
¼ cup raisins
4 cups vegetable stock or water
1 tsp. basil
1 Tbsp. chili powder
2 tsp. cumin powder
1 green pepper, chopped
1 cup tomato paste

Soak dried lentils if you prefer. Drain; add raisins and stock. Simmer 10
minutes. Add other ingredients and simmer 30-45 minutes, until tender,
adding more stock if needed. May be served over rice, noodles or with corn
tortillas.
Serves 6.

To prepare lentil burritos: Heat 2-3 corn tortillas per person in a hot dry
skillet, 30 seconds on a side (just until softened and warm). On top of each
tortilla put ½ cup *Lentils with Love*. Then top each stack with ½ medium
zucchini, shredded, 2 Tbsp. yogurt and 2 Tbsp. fresh alfalfa sprouts.

Embracing Mother Earth

*The amazing list of high-fiber foods includes most of
the major ingredients in this meal: corn, lentils, zucchini, raisins and
tomatoes. So it tones the body while it nurtures us with the love of cooking
meals that satisfy.*
Enjoy!

Raisin Carob Cookies

View of the Whole

*Just like a good thought that you can turn in many directions
and benefit from, these cookies will suit many tastes, many occasions.*

**1¼ cups whole wheat pastry flour
1¼ cups unbleached white flour
⅓ cup carob powder
1 tsp. baking powder
½ tsp. baking soda
½ cup soft butter
1 tsp. vanilla
¾ cup honey
¾ cup yogurt
1 Tbsp. coffee flavor (optional)
1 cup raisins or currants**

Mix dry ingredients in a bowl. In a large bowl, cream butter, then add vanilla
and honey. Mix well, then mix in yogurt and coffee flavor. Add dry
ingredients; stir in raisins. On buttered cookie sheet, drop by small spoonfuls.
Bake 10-15 minutes at 375° until just set. Don't overbake; they will firm as
they cool.
Makes 3-4 dozen.

Options:

Variations on this theme include adding a banana and 1 tsp. cinnamon (and ½ cup
less yogurt), or mint extract instead of vanilla, or adding ½ cup nuts. You can melt
the butter and honey while the oven heats, but this changes the texture of the
cookies. Experiment with which way you like them better.

Embracing Mother Earth

*This makes a great basic recipe, one with infinite variations.
Plan to make some the next time you have visitors from out of town.
It's a good way to send them on their way—with homemade treats to remind
them of the visit and to provide a healthful snack as they travel on.
Enjoy!*

Cream of Broccoli Soup

View of the Whole

*Stems hold up the flowers, yet how little we value their contribution!
One way to rectify matters is to focus on the food value in broccoli stems,
which can make a whole meal in themselves. When we return
to the stems and roots of our thoughts, we can make
a whole inner meal of focused attention to grow new ideas.*

2 cups broccoli stems
½ cup vegetable stock or water
1 cup milk
1 tsp. Dijon mustard
½ cup cheddar cheese
1 tsp. Bragg's Liquid Aminos

Cut broccoli stems into ½ inch pieces. Simmer in stock for 10-15 minutes or until tender. If they're old and tough, peel them after cooking. With young stems, this soup almost makes itself. Purée cooked stems in the blender with cooking water. Return to stove, adding milk (enough to thin the soup to taste), mustard, cheese and liquid aminos. Stir and heat through but do not boil.
Serves 2 generously.

Options:
Spinach stems are also good for soup. Use nutmeg for flavor; omit mustard and cheese.

Embracing Mother Earth

*Instead of throwing away vegetable stems
in favor of their flowery or leafy tops,
it feels good to make use of this part of our most nutritious foods.
Among broccoli's benefits is a growing reputation for preventing cancer.
But it's enough to be simply a healthful green, available almost year round.
Enjoy!*

Easy Banana Bread

View of the Whole

*When making this bread in hot weather, think of the tropics
that sustain us by providing fruits like this that we take for granted.
Remember the people who plant and harvest,
who ship and sell, who spend their lives
nurturing the plants we enjoy.*

½ cup butter (or part unrefined vegetable oil)
½ cup honey
3 cups whole wheat flour
1 tsp. baking powder
½ tsp. cinnamon
1½ cups mashed banana (3-4 ripe bananas)
1 Tbsp. yogurt
½ tsp. baking soda
1 cup nuts, chopped (or part sunflower seeds) (optional)

Melt butter and honey in the oven while it heats to 350°. Add flour, baking powder and cinnamon. Mash bananas and mix with yogurt, baking soda and nuts. Add to other ingredients and mix lightly. Bake in buttered bread pan or 9" x 9" baking pan for 1 hour.
Serves 8-10.

Embracing Mother Earth

*As we learn to focus more on locally grown produce, bananas
take a secondary position in our diets (unless you live in the tropics).
This allows us to pay even more attention to them,
their origin and their journey to reach us,
when we do choose to eat them.
It's all a matter of awareness.
Enjoy!*

Orange Carrot Soup

View of the Whole

*Carrots are like sunshine, bright and warming, nutritious and easy to enjoy.
So why not occasionally make a meal of them? This tasty soup adds another
delight—fresh oranges. Double your sunshine, double your fun. And double
the pleasure of cooking that allows you to enjoy life's treasures.*

**6 carrots, sliced
3 Tbsp. butter
1 Tbsp. nutritional yeast (optional)
1 tsp. thyme (minced, if fresh)
¼ cup fresh parsley, minced
(plus some extra for garnish)
8 cups vegetable stock or water
1 Tbsp. Bragg's Liquid Aminos
juice of one orange, and its peel,
 finely minced
¼ cup cream
black pepper
bay leaf**

Sauté carrots in butter for ten minutes. Add yeast, herbs and stock, and
simmer 25 minutes. Liquefy soup in the blender until smooth. Return to
stove and add orange peel, juice and cream, stirring to combine (but not boil).
Then cover and let it stand for 15 minutes to blend flavors before serving.
Garnish with fresh parsley.
Serves 6-8.

Embracing Mother Earth

*Support local growers and what they produce. Use ingredients
like oranges sparingly, as a special treat like this soup, rather than regularly out
of habit—unless you live where they grow. Simplicity is Nature's trade in stock.
Although her ways may seem complex, underneath is life as simple as this soup,
combining only the ingredients that need to be together to form a complete and
satisfying whole. We have much to learn and to enjoy.*
Soup's on!

Favorite Coffee Cake

View of the Whole

*Like combining recipes, we can also combine our thoughts
about a topic into something creatively better, knowing that this process also
takes awhile to perfect. We're always coming closer.*

½ cup butter
⅓-½ cup honey
1 tsp. cinnamon (at least)
¼ tsp. nutmeg or ginger,
   depending on fruit used
2 cups whole wheat pastry flour
1½ tsp. baking powder
½ tsp. baking soda
1 cup yogurt
½ cup raisins (optional)
2-3 cups fresh fruit, chopped

Melt butter and honey in the oven while heating it to 350°. Meanwhile,
mix dry ingredients together. Add yogurt and raisins to melted butter and
honey; then combine with dry ingredients. In a buttered 9" x 13" baking
dish, put the chopped fruit to make a solid layer on the bottom (amount
depends on juiciness of fruit). Spread the batter on top of the fruit evenly to
the edges of the dish. Top with 1 tsp. cinnamon and 2 Tbsp. honey or brown
sugar, plus chopped nuts if you wish. Bake 30-45 minutes or until well
browned.
Serves 8-12, depending on how many people you have to divide it among.

Options:
Add the grated peel of a lemon or orange and use ⅓ cup sesame seeds in the batter
instead of nuts on top. Any fruit in season is good, including fresh strawberries and/
or rhubarb. The fruit need not be firm, so you can also use fresh-frozen fruits like
blueberries, pie cherries or peaches. Another treat is to use fresh pineapple and 2
Tbsp. honey, 2 tsp. vanilla, add ginger and top with shredded coconut instead of
cinnamon and honey.

Embracing Mother Earth

*She deserves an embrace or at least a mental hug for
this wonderful breakfast treat, dinner dessert or tea break.
Enjoy in every season, any time of day!*

Another Lentil Stew

View of the Whole

*One virtue to have in cooking is flexibility. When winter squash weren't available
to stuff with this lentil concoction, baked potatoes turned out to be just as good,
maybe better. As we stuff our thoughts into words or actions,
it helps even more to be flexible and flow with "what is"
rather than holding to what "should be."*

½ cup dried lentils
vegetable stock or water
1 tsp. Bragg's Liquid Aminos
2 carrots, sliced
2 Tbsp. sunflower seeds
2 Tbsp. shredded cheese (your choice of kinds)
1 Tbsp. wheat germ

Simmer lentils in vegetable stock or water to cover, with the carrots and
liquid aminos, for 45 minutes. Add herbs to taste (cumin is good). Put into
a casserole dish, top with seeds, cheese and wheat germ and bake until
cheese is melted. Do this while the potatoes bake their last 15 minutes.
Serve hot on baked potatoes to 4 waiting people.

Embracing Mother Earth

*Lentil leftovers (if any) can be blended
and used as a sandwich spread.
Enjoy!*

Fresh Ginger Bread

View of the Whole

*Few recipes have the impact of this that brings the
freshness of its ingredients to our immediate awareness. We can learn an
invaluable lesson from this—to keep our thoughts fresh so that their results
in the form of our words and actions, even our dreams, are also fresh and have
an immediate impact.*

5 Tbsp. butter
3 Tbsp. freshly grated ginger root
½ cup honey
½ cup molasses
½ cup yogurt
1 tsp. dry mustard, or Dijon
1½ tsp. baking powder
½ tsp. ground cloves or allspice
½ tsp. cinnamon
¼ tsp. nutmeg
2 cups whole wheat pastry flour

Sauté butter and ginger root together lightly 3-4 minutes. Remove from heat.
Beat together honey and molasses vigorously for 5 minutes. Add ginger
and butter mixture, then yogurt. Mix dry ingredients thoroughly in a large
mixing bowl. Make a well in the middle and add the wet mixture, mixing
thoroughly but minimally. Spread in a well buttered 9" x 9" pan and bake
at 350° for 30-35 minutes, or until a toothpick inserted in the center comes
out clean. It is good plain or with butter or yogurt.
Serves 9.

Embracing Mother Earth

*This will spoil you for any other kind of gingerbread. It's amazingly different
from the packaged versions and is a good example of the value of rediscovering
the joy and ease of cooking with unprocessed ingredients. And plan to make it
again—soon. You are sure to get requests.
Enjoy!*

Sauce to Savor

View of the Whole

*This is a savory to savor, by all means. Its versatility is enhanced
by its simplicity, like most of the truly valuable things in life.*

¾ cup unrefined vegetable oil
1 Tbsp. basil
¾ cup vegetable stock or water
1 Tbsp. oregano
¼ cup Bragg's Liquid Aminos
1 Tbsp. lemon juice
2 Tbsp. nutritional yeast
1 lb. tofu

Mix all ingredients in a blender until smooth and creamy.
Makes about 2 cups, serving 4-6.

Options:
This sauce works well on salads, on Mexican food (good cheese substitute), on
steamed vegetables or Brendas's Baked Tofu (pg. 104). Another possibility is a
topping for baked potatoes, come winter time.

Embracing Mother Earth

*This wonderful concoction is deceptively simple.
It creates even more time for us to spend outdoors
this special time of year. In any of its incarnations,
enjoy!*

Oatmeal Treasures

View of the Whole

Once in awhile a recipe—like an idea—comes through that you know is so simple it quickly becomes a permanent addition to your base of knowledge. "What we focus on expands" was an idea like that in my life.

3 cups oats
1 cup butter
1½ cups whole wheat pastry flour
½ cup honey
½ -1 cup jam

Mix together all ingredients except jam. Spread half of the mixture in a buttered 9" x 13" dish. Spread with jam (amount depends on your taste or the amount of left over jam you're finishing up). Sprinkle remaining mixture over jam, spreading as evenly as possible, and patting it down. Bake at 350° for 25-30 minutes, until light golden brown. When cool, cookies will be firmer; then cut into bars.
Makes 36 bars.

Embracing Mother Earth

This is a great way to share jam on more than toast, especially homemade jam with full fruit flavor. You can mix different kinds as well, so it's also a good way to finish off those ends of jam jars (unless your children already do that for you).
Enjoy!

Spring Tonic

View of the Whole

*Something in our makeup knows when it's spring and the body is in need of a
pick-me-up of fresh greens. Here's a satisfying way to accommodate that need,
a reminder for the palate of what we also know intuitively with the mind:
Freshness creates new energy from ancient inner wisdom.*

**8 cups kale, chopped
or 12 cups chard, chopped
1 cup celery, sliced
2 Tbsp. unrefined vegetable oil
(or half butter)
1 tsp. dried dill weed
½ cup cottage cheese
1 Tbsp. fresh lemon juice
2 Tbsp. yogurt**

Steam greens in a small amount of vegetable stock or water until tender,
approximately 5 minutes; drain. Sauté celery in oil. Blend other ingredients;
add celery and toss mixture with greens. Can be used as a side dish, or as
a main dish with steamed brown rice.
Serves 4-6.

Embracing Mother Earth

*If any kale or chard wintered over in the garden, add a few leaves to freshen the
pot. Even if it's not noticeable by the other eaters, you will know it's there
and honor it all the more for having been grown close to home. If you didn't
plant one of these easy-to-grow vegetables, consider it for the
coming season or for next fall.
Enjoy!*

Fresh Raspberry Pie

View of the Whole

Raspberries are good just as they are picked, but this pie allows you to enjoy them fresh in a special form if you want to play. We can create such specialness about any aspect of our lives, just by deciding to "play" a little. And it's more fun!

3 cups raspberries
2 cups fresh apple juice
2 Tbsp. agar flakes

Create a Walnut Crust (pg. 19). Bake unfilled at 350° for 10-12 minutes, until lightly browned. When crust is cool, fill to the brim with fresh raspberries. Heat fresh apple juice until it boils. Stir in agar flakes and simmer 5 minutes, stirring to melt flakes. Cool 30 minutes. Pour apple juice mixture over raspberries. Chill pie several hours until firm. Serve plain, with plain yogurt, or with Whipped Tofu.

Whipped Tofu

½ cup tofu
½ cup plain yogurt
1 Tbsp. maple syrup or honey

Combine ingredients in the blender until smooth. That's all there is to it.
Makes 1 cup

Embracing Mother Earth

Freshness is the key.
Eating fresh foods—especially raw foods—is especially good
for our health: physical, mental and spiritual. Enjoy the benefits
of all of these, and treat yourself well. You deserve it!
Enjoy!

Greenery—Spinach with Lentils

View of the Whole

*It's time to rediscover both lentils and spinach,
easily and tastily. And we learn to dance between dried ingredients
and fresh, just as we combine old memories and new experiences into the
wholeness that is our being.*

1 cup dry lentils
3 cups vegetable stock or water
1 large bunch of fresh spinach,
  chopped including stems
½ tsp. ground cumin
½ tsp. ground coriander
freshly ground black pepper
3 Tbsp. butter
2 Tbsp. chopped fresh parsley

Cover lentils with water and soak overnight, if you prefer. Drain (save the water for your plants!) and cover with 3 cups of vegetable stock or fresh water. Simmer 30 minutes; set aside.

Melt butter in large skillet over medium heat. Add spinach stems and cook 2 minutes, until stems soften. Add the rest of the spinach and cook until it wilts, about 2 more minutes. Add lentils (save cooking liquid for soup) and other ingredients and stir just until heated through; do not overcook. *Serves 4. (If it's the main dish for hungry people, consider using more spinach.)*

Embracing Mother Earth

*We can become more conscious of all the ingredients we use,
not simply the beans and vegetables. The soaking water from beans is very
nutritious for house and garden plants. And the change of water helps to
reduce the discomfort some feel after eating beans. That side effect, by the
way, lessens when you eat beans regularly. The cooking liquid is also very
nutritious, and improves the flavor and value of other cooking. (Add it
consciously, however. Some vegetable flavors might not fit comfortably in a
dessert recipe.) Buy your ingredients just as consciously as you cook them. If you
consider the overall cost of a meal, organically grown vegetables add very little.
However, they add considerably to your consciousness of eating well-grown food,
and their purchase supports those who choose to grow food in that philosophy.
Enjoy!*

Everything Plus Carob Cookies

View of the Whole

When you want to enjoy cookies to the fullest, find a recipe like this one that includes as many favorite ingredients as possible. It's the same in everything we do: to enjoy it to the fullest, we bring in all our favorite ingredients.

¾ cup butter
¾ cup honey
1 tsp. vanilla
1 cup whole wheat flour
½ tsp. baking soda
3 cups oats
2 cups carob chips
1 cup finely grated coconut

Mix butter and honey, but do not melt butter first. (Otherwise it melts the carob chips). Add vanilla, then flour and baking soda. Mix well, then add oats, chips and coconut; mix again. Drop by small spoonfuls on a buttered cookie sheet. Bake at 350° for 10-12 minutes.
Makes 4-5 dozen.

Embracing Mother Earth

*While honoring these cookies the first time I made them,
I envisioned the fruit of the tree (coconut), the fruit of the bush
(carob), the fruit of the grain (oats and wheat) and the fruit of the bees'
labor (honey). These became a bouquet I offered, symbolizing the unique
aspects of each of us that together make up the whole
delicious result of who we are.
Enjoy!*

Cream of Fresh Pea Soup

View of the Whole

*Shared long ago by a friend, this gourmet treat is so
simple that you have to try it to believe it. Mint is the secret ingredient.
What secret flavoring do you enjoy spicing your life with? It pays to focus on
that and smile as you discover your own inner resources.*

2 cups fresh (or frozen) peas
6-8 fresh mint leaves
1 cup half-and-half cream
1 Tbsp. butter
1 cup (or more) milk

To peas, add fresh mint leaves. Steam lightly 5 minutes. Liquefy peas and
mint in the blender, adding cream as needed. Reheat gently (do not boil),
with butter and milk to achieve the soup consistency you prefer.
Serves 4.

Options:
If you're fortunate to have edible pea pods in your garden, add some for texture and
don't liquefy them.

Embracing Mother Earth

*This soup creates a delightful supper, especially with
some fresh bread or muffins. The recipe originated with Henri Charpentier, the
famous French chef who invented Crepes Suzettes. According to Barbara, the
friend who shared this recipe, he said, "serving peas just plain cooked
bespoke lack of imagination."
Enjoy!*

Muffins in a Pan

View of the Whole

Why should lack of a muffin tin dissuade you from enjoying muffins?
You can spread this batter in a pizza pan or in a 9" x 13" baking dish.
It tastes just as good—and those sharing it can cut as big a piece as they
want, rather than your assigning everyone the same muffin-sized appetite.
We each have our own appetite. Cooking is a good way to notice what
entices ours and to pay more attention to how we respond, creating new
ways to satisfy our inner selves and not just our stomachs.

2 cups whole wheat flour
2 tsp. baking powder
¼ cup sunflower seeds
2 Tbsp. sesame seeds
¼ cup honey
¼ cup unrefined vegetable oil
1¼ cups milk

Combine dry ingredients. Mix in wet ingredients quickly. Pour into a buttered baking pan. Bake at 400° approximately 20 minutes or until it sounds done (doesn't talk back when you put your ear to the pan and listen to it closely).
Serves 4.

Options:
You can sprinkle sesame seeds on top before baking, or use almonds or walnuts instead (or as part of the amount) of sunflower seeds.

Embracing Mother Earth

A simple bread brings simple joy and adds a special touch to any meal.
On warm days, bake late at night so the house can cool before morning.
Leave the bread at room temperature and enjoy both the cooler house
and the special supper it helps to create.
Enjoy!

Sauce for Anything (well, almost)

View of the Whole

What starts as an invention for one purpose may out do itself when you consider other uses. Seldom are our thoughts serving only one purpose either, and we can benefit by remembering how wide-ranging our thoughts may be.

4 cups tomato purée
8-12 mushrooms, sliced
1 tsp. chili powder
1 Tbsp. carob powder
1 tsp. Bragg's Liquid Aminos
1 tsp. decaffeinated coffee (optional)
¼ cup raisins
1 tsp. cumin powder
3 carrots, cut in thin rounds
12 corn tortillas
Toppings (see suggestions)

Mix all ingredients except tortillas and toppings; simmer 10-15 minutes. If the sauce is too thin, dissolve 1-2 Tbsp. cornstarch in ½ cup cold vegetable stock or water and add, stirring until thick.

Heat the tortillas one at a time in a hot dry skillet. On a plate, top hot tortilla with your favorite toppings (let eaters each choose their own). Add sauce and repeat layers, topping the dish off with sour cream, yogurt or avocado cubes.
Serves 4-6.

Options:
Suggested toppings include cooked black (or other) beans, shredded lettuce, chopped tomato, sunflower seeds and whatever else strikes your fancy. You can add chopped olives, green chili or other delectables to the bubbling sauce. It can be served over rice, baked potatoes, pasta or beans.

Embracing Mother Earth

*This recipe grew organically as I added dashes of this
and that while conversing with a visiting friend. I don't know if it's a cross
between an enchilada and a taco, a burrito, or just me but it has endless
variations one can muse over—and
enjoy!*

Easy Banana Pudding

View of the Whole

*This simple dessert takes little heat. We can keep our thoughts cool by choosing
to focus on ones that give us little internal heat. Combining the pudding with
candy from the garden makes the meal even more special.
Hummingbirds whiz through the comfrey flowers at the moment, but all too often
we forget it's there for us to use as well. How typical of us humans to forget the
bounty that surrounds us! Good thing we have the hummies to remind us.*

¾ cup shredded coconut
¼ cup unrefined vegetable oil
1 lb. tofu
½ cup honey
2 bananas
1 tsp. vanilla

Heat coconut in a dry heavy skillet, stirring constantly, until lightly browned.
Set aside. In a blender, mix other ingredients until smooth. It may help to
do this half at a time, depending on your blender. Stir in coconut.
Serves 4-6.

Comfrey Root Candy

2 Tbsp. grated comfrey root
2 Tbsp. finely grated coconut
1 Tbsp. carob powder
2 Tbsp. honey

Dig enough pieces of comfrey root (they have lots to spare if your plants are
more than a year in place) to make 2 Tbsp. when grated. Wash well and
grate. Mix with grated coconut, carob powder and honey. Let it sit to congeal
and mingle the flavors. Roll into small balls.
Makes 6-8 small balls, enough for just a taste.

Embracing Mother Earth

*This pudding recipe comes from Surata Soyfoods in
Eugene, Oregon, who promote a variety of ways to use tofu. The coconut gives
the pudding a texture that's more appealing to those who aren't familiar with
tofu—yet. As a healing agent and blood purifier, comfrey perks up your
constitution, and this candy is a great conversation piece.
Enjoy!*

Pasta with Mustard Butter

View of the Whole

*It's wonderful to have a few standard recipes with infinite
possibilities, and this may well become one for you as it is now for me. Our
minds can use a few such standards as well—those positive affirmations that we
can call on any time with infinite possibilities. Mixing up this delightful
dinner dish gives good occasion to call such thoughts to mind.*

¼ cup each butter and unrefined vegetable oil
¼ cup Dijon mustard
¼ cup chopped parsley
1 Tbsp. miso (optional) or Bragg's Liquid Aminos
1 Tbsp. vegetable oil
2 cups broccoli, cut in small pieces
4 Tbsp. vegetable stock or water
¾ lb. pasta (corn spaghetti is good)

Combine butter, oil, mustard, parsley and miso in a small pan, and heat until melted together and warmed. Meanwhile, in a large skillet, steam-fry broccoli by heating 1 Tbsp. oil. Add chopped broccoli and vegetable stock or water. Cover and steam on high heat five minutes or until hot but still crisp.

Cook pasta in a large pan of boiling water until tender (7-10 minutes for whole wheat, 5-7 minutes for corn). Drain and rinse with hot water. Toss with sauce and broccoli.
Serves 4.

Options:

For variety, you may include some small pieces of cauliflower, slivers of carrot or replace broccoli with summer squash or peas. If tomatoes are used—such as cherry tomatoes cut in halves—add them with the mustard butter.

Embracing Mother Earth

*Bright colors signal the coming summer season.
This easy pasta gives us extra time to spend in the garden
or simply to look out the window. Go outside now and touch the Earth,
if you can, to remember our connection and our foods',
and feel that connection inside yourself.
Enjoy!*

Zen Blueberry Soup

View of the Whole

*One taster dubbed this soup a meditation in itself. It's
an honor to the soup—and the eater—to consider food this way and a practice
we can all do more often, more beneficially. Simply pause a moment to consider
its source, our own and the use to which we put the food.*

2 cups blueberries
¼ cup freshly squeezed orange juice
¼ tsp. allspice
¼ tsp. nutmeg
yogurt

Into a blender put blueberries, juice, allspice and nutmeg; blend at low speed.
Chill until serving time. Serve with yogurt on top, garnished with a half-slice
of fresh orange or a few borage (or other garden edible) flowers.
Serves 4.

Options:
During blueberry season, this is a winner. In early spring, before the berries have
even flowered, it's a great way to use the last of the ones frozen last season. Because
the berries are blended, the soup doesn't need plump firm berries.

Embracing Mother Earth

*What more can I say than—
enjoy!*

As Others Say It

Comments by some other writers whose philosophy complements that of this book are shared below. These are direct quotes [unless bracketed, which indicates my notes], but the thoughts in each paragraph are excerpted and not necessarily sequential in the original writings.

Bo Lozoff in *We're All Doing Time*:

Genuine changes, deep changes in our relationship to food, usually require conscious effort. It's spiritual work, just like yoga or meditation. The best time for this work is *before and during each meal*. Without drawing much attention to yourself, take a minute or so before eating to:

1. Get calm and centered.

2. Look at the food on your plate and realize that all of its energy came ultimately from the Sun; vegetables grow from sun-power, . . . [and] all food-energy ultimately comes from sun energy, which is pure LIGHT.

3. Instruct your body to be receptive to this Light, and not to worry about the rest.

4. Rather than feeling "resigned" about eating this food, give thanks instead, because dealing with this teaching is bound to increase your wisdom and power.

5. Pay attention as you eat, consciously consuming this food for perfect physical and spiritual health. If possible eat alone for awhile so you can concentrate better.

Even if all of this sounds corny to you, trust it just long enough to see how it feels. After all, doesn't it make more sense than to go on cursing the food that you eat? [*Directed to a prison inmate dealing with prison food*].

Elson M. Hass, M.D. in *Staying Healthy with the Seasons*:

What is it that no one can live without, and that everyone wants more of? It is *energy*, both physical and mental. We spend time, dollars, and energy itself looking for it. Your life force ("chi" or "prana") depends on sunlight, clean air, pure water, good food, and sleep. The highest life force comes from unsullied nature, eating as close to the garden as possible while the sun, air, and water are still circulating in your food. Smaller quantities of good quality foods help you more than gorging on lower quality foods. Foods are fuels which heat the body, and balance your activity with the heat or coldness of each season. I do not feel the quality of animal foods is as good for you as the vegetable world's, but this choice is up to each individual's discretion and wisdom. Overeating or eating when upset affects your vital energy as much as eating poor foods. Eating light, wholesome foods prepared with love in a comfortable setting will nourish you completely.

Starhawk in *Truth or Dare*:

When making money becomes a substitute for foraging, gathering, hunting, planting, we lose important sources of power. The zucchini I buy in the store with money is entirely different from the one I pluck off the vine in my garden. The store-bought squash is an object, a dismembered part of the dead world, while the one in my garden is a whole process in which I have participated, from the composting of my garbage to the sense of wonder evoked when I find the vine still producing in November. I am not suggesting that we all turn to subsistence farming, but that our sense of self-worth is dependent on some direct contact with the broader cycles of birth, growth, death, decay, and renewal that do, in reality, sustain our lives. For even Hostess Twinkies are made of flour made of grain, and time still moves in its cycles and seasons even when tracked by a digital clock.

To heal ourselves, to create a sustainable culture, we must consider how we meet our needs: the needs of the individual body and of the larger earth-body that encompasses us all.

Stuart Silverstein in *Bread in Time—Breadbaking Without Angst*:

Just bake your bread[s] quietly and joyfully and I guarantee they will be good for you.

Carol J. Adams in *The Sexual Politics of Meat: A Feminist— Vegetarian Critical Theory*:

Meat is king: this noun describing meat is a noun denoting male power. Vegetables, a generic term meat eaters use for all foods that are not meat, have become as associated with women as meat is with men, recalling on a subconscious level the days of Woman the Gatherer. Since women have been made subsidiary in a male-dominated, meat-eating world, so has our food. The foods associated with second-class citizens are considered to be second-class protein. Just as it is thought a woman cannot make it on her own, so we think that vegetables cannot make a meal on their own, despite the fact that meat is only secondhand vegetables and vegetables provide, on the average, more than twice the vitamins and minerals of meat.

The coining of this word [vegetarian] has caused a conflict in interpretation about its etymology. *The Oxford English Dictionary* states that the name is derived irregularly from "Veget-able" plus "arian." Vegetarians hold to a different etymology. They argue that it is "from the Latin word *vegetus*, meaning 'whole, sound, fresh or lively,' as in the ancient Latin term *homo vegetus*—a mentally and physically vigorous person. Thus, the English vegetarians were trying to make a point about the philosophical and moral tone of the lives they sought to lead. They were not simply promoting the use of vegetables in the diet." [quoting Vic Sussman, *The Vegetarian Alternative: A Guide to a Healthful and Humane Diet*, Emmaus, PA, Rodale Press, 1978].

Dr. Henry G. Bieler in *Food Is Your Best Medicine*:

Vegetables should be steamed, preferably, or cooked in small amounts of water. Overcooking destroys enzymes and vitamins. Always use the cooking water, either in soups or as a drink.

Remember that the volatile oils and other irritants found in onions, radishes, garlic, scallions, watercress, sharp-tasting salad greens, most spices and peelings with bitter flavors are poisons that nature puts into those plants to discourage the attacking insects. Spices, then, are natural insecticides and therefore not edible, although often stimulating and appetite-whetting. But since these volatile oils may irritate the delicate kidney tubules, they should be eliminated from the diet. To those who use gourmet French cookbooks this will came as sad news; nevertheless, many of my colleagues and I believe it to be the truth.

Dr. M. Ted Morter, Jr. in *Your Health Your Choice*:

[His "wellness principles" include the following:] The conscious mind of man is no match for the Intelligence Within. Too much protein leads to toxicity. Eating feeds more than our bodies. In the body, everything affects everything else.

In the split second of fertilization, there is perfection! Instantly, perfection is expressed. From that split second of perfection comes a perfect human being, unless something interferes. Development may be less than perfect when the environment is not conducive to supporting the perfection that was created. Although perfection is flawless, it is not indestructible. It can be overridden when the contrivances of man's educated mind (including conscious selection of inappropriate food) interfere. Nevertheless, we were all perfect when we started out! At conception, we all had our split second of perfection . . . . The same perfect intelligence that was present at conception guides the body's functions throughout life. It doesn't desert us or float off into the ionosphere when we are born. It keeps functioning instant by instant to keep us alive. Our internal intelligence keeps us going despite all of the abuse we heap on ourselves. *The body never makes a mistake.*

Any substance that interferes with the natural workings of the body is a toxin—food included!

Thoughts exert the most powerful influence on your health, and *negative thoughts are the #1 acid producer in your body.*

The members of the lowly plant kingdom may not be able to compute sums or build bridges or philosophize, but they can do something that man, in his finite wisdom, cannot: they can break the nearly inseparable ionic bonds of the mineral kingdom. Plants can take minerals from the soil, break the strong bonds, and incorporate the minerals into their physical beings.

Nature combines the plant and mineral kingdoms in the presence of sunlight through the process of photosynthesis. The food we eat should come from the plant kingdom. It is the source of food that the body can utilize most efficiently. We are able to use minerals that have been processed through the plant kingdom because of the way the atoms or ions of these elements are bonded.

Plants also provide other elements essential for complete nutrition—enzymes and vitamins. Enzymes are the complex proteins that stimulate chemical reactions. When plants are eaten, the enzymes contained in the plants assist the digestive system in processing the food of which they are a part. Without enzymes, food is "dead." The more food is commercially processed, the fewer enzymes it has.

Whole foods have the ingredients to spark responses that bring about more than survival. When you choose foods that serve your body best, you choose health.

Patricia Robinett in *The Runoff*:

Vitamin B12 is present in the flesh of animals and in vegetable foods. But most important, B12 is normally produced inside our bodies by healthy intestines.

The 1959 United States Department of Agriculture Yearbook report explained that putrefaction in the intestines hampers the secretion of "intrinsic factor," necessary for the production of B12. Experts agree that excess protein and refined foods are the main sources of putrefaction in the intestines.

Obviously, the most important safeguard against B12 deficiency is to take good care of the intestines.

What are food sources of B12? . . . seaweed and algae; bee pollen; brewer's yeast; aged soy sauce and/or tamari, tempeh, miso; wheat, barley or alfalfa juice, dark green leafy vegetables; organically grown root vegetables and ginseng. Perhaps their B12 content is one reason why these foods are celebrated worldwide as especially healthful.

B12 deficiency is an important issue. It is so important that *The American Journal of Psychiatry* warns that psychiatric symptoms may be the first indications of vitamin B12 deficiency and recommends blood tests for B12 deficiency in all patients with psychiatric symptoms.

Could it be that a simple B vitamin deficiency may contribute to the mental extremes exhibited by mothers during pregnancy and after birth, hyperactive children, the aged, or by others?

Svevo Brooks in *The Art of Good Living—Simple Steps to Regaining Health and the Joy of Life*:

Quite obviously we are what we eat, and a lot more. In fact, one could easily argue that what we do with the fuel—how we assimilate and eliminate it—is even more important than what we put in. A very calm person, for example, will utilize her or his food better than a very tense person.

As we grow older we begin foraging for food, in fields, gardens and supermarkets. Even after we gather the food, there are conscious acts involved with using it as fuel: we must prepare it, peel it, wash it, cook it, etc. and then put it into our mouths. This actual picking up of the food with our hands and putting it into our mouths is what makes the food experience so special. It makes our relationship to food both intimate and personal, a relationship that is unique among body fuels.

What Is a Vegetarian? by the Brahma Kumaris World Spiritual Organization:

The relationship between the mind and the body is an important and delicate one. The knowledge of gourmet recipes is not necessarily the key to becoming a great cook.

The kind of thoughts we have during the preparation of our food has a very real effect on its constitution, and thus, indirectly, on our own mental and physical processes. Plants are known to respond to a kind, loving atmosphere; in the same way, whilst dealing with food, we should pay attention that we are spreading the vibrations of elevated, positive thoughts. Then, when we take that food in, it has a beneficial effect on both mind and body.

In spiritual circles, it is considered more important that food has been prepared with love and offered to God than that it is time-consumingly presented or varied.

Darcy Williamson and Lisa Railsback in *Cooking with Spirit—North American Indian Food and Fact*:

[The native cooks in this country] did not eat for sheer pleasure; they ate to survive, they ate what the land offered, and they seasoned their food with spirit.

Even with the drastic changes in environment and lifestyles the North American Indians have undergone, attitudes in preparation of foods and choice of utensils remains important. As is traditional, foods are acquired with reverence and attention to its importance in the balance of nature. Each animal, fish or plant has unique qualities and powers, and are considered a relative to all life. When any are eaten, used or worn, these qualities become part of the person utilizing them. Even utensils, weapons and tools are channels of spirit energy, positive or negative, which can be passed to foods and material goods.

Harmony with nature is always important. Water flows clockwise and one must stir food in a clockwise direction. To flow with nature is survival. To remember that all life, plant and animal, should be regarded with reverence, is survival.

The attitude of persons preparing food is extremely important, also. A happy, peaceful cook is healthful, while anger or negative feelings cause inferior foods or illness. Love of one's family means joy in cooking.

Author's Postscript

Cooking in peace—with peace—creates an atmosphere of peace in which we can grow more fully. As we become more peaceful cooks, so do our lives become more peaceful. This is not a bland peace, but the spice of life. It is the ultimate challenge to create, which in itself creates the ultimate joy.

Like us
our Mother Earth
is born
from the womb of darkness
the primordial night

Like her
we sing of springtime
of rebirth
of all the seasons
as they turn

Like her
we smoke the pipe of peace
in mists upon the mountains
and rain blessings
on all the directions

Like all beings
we carry within us
the seeds
to express
the freedom
of life
wit

—h.k.

Index